The Exceptional Teacher's Handbook

Third Edition

Carla dedicates the third edition to her husband, Drew, for his continued love and inspiration as she follows her dreams. She thanks her sisters, Joyce Kelley and Jennifer Walsh, for their infinite words of encouragement as she continues her work in the education profession.

The Exceptional Teacher's Handbook

Third Edition

The First-Year Special Education Teacher's Guide to Success

Carla F. Shelton
Alice B. Pollingue

CORWIN
A SAGE Company

For information:

Corwin
A SAGE Company
2455 Teller Road
Thousand Oaks, California 91320
(800) 233-9936
Fax: (800) 417-2466
www.corwinpress.com

SAGE India Pvt. Ltd.
B 1/I 1 Mohan Cooperative
    Industrial Area
Mathura Road, New Delhi 110 044
India

SAGE Ltd.
1 Oliver's Yard
55 City Road
London EC1Y 1SP
United Kingdom

SAGE Asia-Pacific Pte. Ltd.
33 Pekin Street #02-01
Far East Square
Singapore 048763

Printed in the United States of America.

Library of Congress Cataloging-in-Publication Data

Shelton, Carla F.
The exceptional teacher's handbook: the first-year special education teacher's guide to success/Carla F. Shelton and Alice B. Pollingue.—3rd ed.
        p. cm.
Includes bibliographical references and index.
ISBN 978-1-4129-6913-0 (cloth)
ISBN 978-1-4129-6914-7 (pbk.)

    1. Special education—United States—Handbooks, manuals, etc. 2. Special education teachers—United States—Handbooks, manuals, etc. 3. First year teachers—United States—Handbooks, manuals, etc. I. Pollingue, Alice B. II. Title.

LC3969.S36 2009
371.9'0973—dc22   2008044784

This book is printed on acid-free paper.

13 14 15 16 17 10 9 8 7 6 5 4 3

Acquisitions Editor:	David Chao
Editorial Assistant:	Brynn Saito
Production Editor:	Amy Schroller
Copy Editor:	Kristin Bergstad
Typesetter:	C&M Digitals (P) Ltd.
Proofreader:	Jennifer Gritt
Indexer:	Jean Casalegno
Cover Designer:	Rose Storey
Graphic Designer:	Karine Hovsepian

Contents

Preface

The *Exceptional Teacher's Handbook* is a comprehensive resource book designed to assist and support the special education teacher through his or her first school year and new teaching experience. The handbook supplies the first-year teacher with a step-by-step guide designed to improve and enhance his or her skills in the areas of planning, organization, and time management. This resource book contains information on critical and timely topics such as differentiation, discipline, transition, RTI and progress monitoring, alternate assessments, classroom organization and design, parent conferences, and professional learning. In addition, the authors have included resources that supply the new teacher with a wealth of miscellaneous information, beginning with emergencies in the school setting and concluding with a glossary of current education terminology.

The purpose of the *Exceptional Teacher's Handbook* is to provide the first-year special education teacher with the tools necessary to make the transformation from novice to professional successfully. The authors recognize that a tremendous amount of diversity exists among special education programs and delivery models; however, the basic concepts presented throughout the book can be applied to most situations. The authors encourage the reader to utilize the book as a resource and guide as he or she begins to chart a course toward a successful first year.

The third edition of *The Exceptional Teacher's Handbook* has been revised to address the most common needs of beginning special education teachers as identified by current research. The authors have added innovative strategies, provided current information pertaining to No Child Left Behind and IDEA 2004, and identified best practices that are utilized by master teachers. The revisions are based on new developments in the education profession and feedback from professionals in the field of special education who have reviewed the second edition. The handbook's contents are sequentially arranged in order to guide the new teacher from the initial planning stage prior to the start of school through the postplanning stage of the school year. The authors provide numerous time-saving checklists and miscellaneous forms that can be reproduced and will assist the beginning teacher in accomplishing the multitude of tasks that are always in existence. The handbook is designed to be utilized as a quick reference; therefore, every chapter is written in an abbreviated format and can be reviewed in a matter of minutes. The chapters are structured in a manner that will provide the reader with current information on the chapter's topic, which is validated by research for most topics, and followed by a plan of action for the teacher when appropriate.

Finally, *The Exceptional Teacher's Handbook* provides the beginning teacher with the necessary framework for a successful school year and will assist the first-year teacher in successfully navigating the ever-changing maze of the special education profession. The handbook was written from a classroom teacher's perspective and supplies the reader with practical suggestions. The contents of the book can be tailored to fit the individual needs of most special education programs or models. The handbook is an indispensable resource that will guide and assist the new teacher throughout the entire school year. More important, the text will empower the first-year special education teacher with the confidence necessary to meet the challenge of the profession.

Acknowledgments

Corwin Press gratefully acknowledges the contributions of the following reviewers:

Kristle F. Evans
Director of Human Resources/Community Relations
Lampeter-Strasburg School District
Lampeter, Pennsylvania

Phyllis N. Levert
College Teaching; School Administrator
Clark Atlanta University; Georgia School Districts
Atlanta, Georgia

Cindy Miller
Program/Project Coordinator
University of North Texas
Denton, Texas

The authors thank the reviewers for their time and efforts on the revision of the third edition of *The Exceptional Teacher's Handbook*. Their feedback served as the authors' beacon throughout the endeavor. The authors would also like to take this opportunity to thank the editors and support staff at Corwin Press for supporting their efforts to provide teachers with quality resources.

About the Authors

Carla F. Shelton, Ed.S., has twenty years of experience in the education profession. The majority of her work has been as a special education teacher where she taught students with disabilities in Grades 2 through 12 in resource, self-contained, and collaborative settings. Carla is certified in the areas of Specific Learning Disability, Emotional Disturbance, Mild Intellectual Disability, Elementary Education (P–8), School Counseling (P–12), and Educational Leadership and Supervision. Currently, she is a school principal working with students in Grades 6–8. Carla is the coauthor of *Best Practices for Secondary School Counselors.*

Carla is knowledgeable in instructional techniques and best classroom practices that promote and foster student learning. She is skilled in designing and implementing strategies designed to assist students with disabilities in meeting academic and behavior goals and objectives, to build bridges between teachers and parents, and to assist students with the transition process from school to school and to postsecondary endeavors. She has mastered the art of collaboration with general education teachers and staff and works effectively with families of students with disabilities. She has presented at the High Schools That Work Summer Conference, the National Tech Prep Conference, the Georgia School Counselor Conference, the National Association of Secondary School Principals, and the Association for Supervision and Curriculum Development Annual Conference. Finally, Carla's solid education background and broad-based educational experience is the foundation on which the third edition of *The Exceptional Teacher's Handbook* is built.

Alice B. Pollingue, Ed.D., is a tenured assistant professor of education at Augusta State University. She has been teaching at the university for more than fourteen years. Alice received her doctorate degree from the University of Alabama. Currently, she teaches special education courses to undergraduate and graduate students and is the supervising professor for the entire special education teacher-training program. She develops curriculum for new special education courses offered at the university. In addition, Alice is a consultant for school systems in the surrounding area. She has published articles in the *Journal of Early Education* and the *Journal of Special Education.* She is active in both local and national professional organizations. Her motivation, professionalism, knowledge, and expertise make her the perfect coauthor for *The Exceptional Teacher's Handbook.*

As a writing team, the authors bring solid professional credentials and expertise in the field of special education to this project. Carla and Alice's shared beliefs, philosophies, and love for the profession led to the writing of a book that epitomizes their common vision.

Introduction

Beginning the Journey

My heart is singing for joy this morning! A miracle has happened! The light of understanding has shone upon my little pupil's mind, and behold, all things are changed!

—Anne Sullivan

The beginning special education teacher will find his or her first school year to be a time of transformation from novice to professional, and the experiences encountered during this period will be remembered for a lifetime. The metamorphosis from student to teacher finally occurs, and the time comes for the beginning teacher to apply all newly acquired knowledge and skills to his or her first teaching position. New teachers enter the education profession for a multitude of reasons; they usually come with the hope, passion, and determination to somehow make a difference in the lives of their students. The idea of guiding students to the point of where "the light of understanding" begins to shine is the ultimate accomplishment that most teachers strive to achieve at some point during their careers. Unfortunately, the reality is that many teachers never discover the true impact they have had on their students, and this is especially true for special education teachers. The lack of "I made a difference" experiences is one of many realities the first-year special education teacher may encounter during his or her new teaching experience. In the information that follows, the authors share with the beginning special education teacher some of the most common concerns and needs of new teachers as found in the current education literature and research for the purpose of validating the teacher's own feelings and preparing him or her for the realities of the first position. In addition, the authors have also found that new teachers often seek the necessary knowledge and skills to become a successful and/or an effective teacher but frequently have no idea how to accomplish this goal. The authors provide the new teacher with general information pertaining to the qualities and characteristics of effective teachers in the latter part of this introduction, and specific strategies in the remainder of the book in an effort to ensure that the reader has the necessary framework to become an effective teacher.

The journey through the first year is often filled with a tremendous amount of promise and excitement, but also frequently contains numerous concerns and unforeseen challenges that will threaten to dampen the new teacher's spirit, dedication, and enthusiasm for the profession and could possibly overshadow the most positive aspects of the first-year experience. All beginning teachers, both special and general, will experience some sort of difficulty during the first year. Mandel (2006) states in his article, "What New Teachers Really Need," the primary concerns of new teachers are "setting up the classroom and preparing for the first weeks of school; covering the required curriculum without falling behind or losing student interest; grading fairly; dealing with parents; and maintaining personal sanity" (p. 67). Gordon and Maxey (2000, p. 6) found the following to be the most common needs of first-year general education teachers:

- Managing the classroom
- Acquiring information about the school system
- Obtaining instructional materials and resources
- Planning, organizing, and managing instruction and other professional responsibilities
- Assessing students and evaluating student progress
- Motivating students
- Using effective teaching methods
- Dealing with individual student's needs, interests, abilities, and problems
- Communicating with colleagues, including administrators, supervisors, and other the teachers
- Communicating with parents
- Adjusting to the teaching environment and role
- Receiving emotional support

Current studies reveal that first-year special education teachers share some of the same concerns as first-year general education teachers. Whitaker (2001) states,

Beginning special education teachers needed assistance in the following areas (from greatest reported need to least reported need): system information related to special education, emotional support, system information related to the school, materials, curriculum, and instruction, discipline, interactions with others, and management. (p. 5)

The statute changes in the Individuals with Disabilities Education Improvement Act and the strict requirements and expectations of the No Child Left Behind Act are additional issues that new teachers are finding extremely intimidating and the source of tremendous stress. These issues are factors that could profoundly impact the decisions of first-year special education teachers to continue in the profession. In the chapters that follow, the authors provide the new special education teacher with specific strategies that target the most common concerns and challenges of not only new teachers, but more specifically, those of first-year special education teachers.

Beginning teachers often spend their first year defining themselves as professionals and perfecting their basic skills as classroom teachers. "How can I become an effective teacher?" is a question that new teachers frequently ask as they journey through their first year. The authors contend that effective teachers, regardless of area of certification, must possess the following in order to develop a culture of learning in their classrooms and promote the academic achievement for all students:

- excellent time management and organizational skills,
- an in-depth understanding of students' needs,
- the ability to manage the classroom and create a climate that promotes student learning,
- the knowledge of best instructional practices that result in an increase in students' academic performances and acquisition of essential skills,
- the ability to prepare students for transition to the next level of education or experiences, and
- the initiative to design and implement a personal, professional learning plan that assists the teacher in staying current in his or her field.

In addition, a study of excellent first-year teachers found these individuals to possess the following defining characteristics:

1. Genuine concern regarding the welfare of their students

2. Commitment to the success of all children

3. Enduring enthusiasm

4. Consistently encouraging attitude

5. Resolve to not be intimidated by challenges (Daugherty, 2003, p. 459)

Teaching is an art that the new teacher is not typically expected to perfect during his or her first year. However, the first-year teacher will be heading in the right direction once he or she obtains a thorough understanding of what it takes to be an effective teacher.

The contents of *The Exceptional Teacher's Handbook* will assist the new teacher in his or her efforts to address the challenges and concerns identified in this introduction. The authors also provide the reader with critical information pertaining to best instructional and classroom practices that will assist the new teacher in developing the qualities and characteristics found in effective teachers. The authors encourage the reader to use the book as a resource and guide as he or she begins to chart a course toward a successful first year.

Preparing for a Successful School Year

Patience, persistence and perspiration make an unbeatable combination for success.

—Napoleon Hill (1883–1970)

Patience, persistence, perspiration, and preparation are the keys to achieving a successful school year for the new special education teacher. The work habits and time management skills that beginning teachers employ during the first days of school set the tone for the remainder of the year. Traditionally, school systems begin the new school year with a preplanning time period designed to provide the opportunity for teachers to prepare for instruction, collaborate with colleagues, participate in professional learning opportunities, and chart a general direction for the upcoming year. Frequently, the new special education teacher must use this time period to confirm his or her new class rosters, resolve transportation issues, coordinate with related service providers, select teachers for students in general education settings, collaborate and plan with general education teachers, create or fine-tune students' schedules, select appropriate instructional materials, and create a class schedule that is conducive to the school's master schedule. The beginning teacher can often be found asking the question, "Where do I begin?"

In the sections that follow, the authors identify six strategies that they have found to be the building blocks for a successful school year. The authors discuss each strategy and provide the reader with the necessary supporting forms and checklists for successful implementation. The chapter includes basic information that will guide the teacher in his or her efforts to address matters ranging from how to familiarize oneself with his or her new school to establishing an effective communication system. The beginning teacher will discover that although each school year is unique, preparation is always the constant element that is critical for a successful and productive year.

STRATEGY 1: GET TO KNOW YOUR SCHOOL

Most school systems will have general orientation sessions for new hires prior to the start of the school year. These sessions generally include a welcome address by the system's superintendent or director of schools, an introduction of support personnel, specific information pertaining to employee benefits and payroll, an orientation to the teacher evaluation program, and an overview of the school system's demographic information and tests results. While these sessions are important, getting to know his or her new school must be a priority for the beginning teacher. The first step the teacher should take once securing his or her first position is to schedule an appointment with the school's principal. The principal can provide the beginning teacher with critical information pertaining to the school's basic framework. Typically, schools have a vision and/or mission statement that defines the school's primary focus; a school improvement plan that lists the goals and objectives designed to increase the school's effectiveness; an Adequate Yearly Progress report that reveals the status of the school in meeting the requirements of the No Child Left Behind Act; and other historical documents and information that can provide the beginning teacher with a basic understanding of the school's journey or "story." The teacher should take this opportunity to request an advance copy of the school's faculty and staff handbook, a copy of the student handbook, a list of the school's extracurricular activities and organizations, and to ask the principal specific questions pertaining to his or her expectations of faculty and staff members and a list of all professional learning opportunities for teachers. Finally, the new teacher should use the appointment time to get acquainted with the school facility and obtain general information about the current faculty and staff. A school yearbook is an excellent resource to assist the new teacher's efforts in becoming familiar his or her new school and colleagues. The authors have a created a checklist that the beginning teacher can use as guide during the meeting.

Materials or Resources

Form 1.1 Get to Know Your School Checklist

STRATEGY 2: ALLOCATE TIME FOR REFLECTING

The first-year special education teacher should allocate a sufficient amount of time for personal reflection throughout the school year. The authors recommend that the teacher maintain a journal to record daily or weekly thoughts and feelings pertaining to his or her school experiences. The teacher will find this exercise to be one that not only relieves stress but also can provide insight into classroom practices that prove to be productive and identify those that definitely need to be "tweaked." In addition to maintaining a journal, the authors recommend that the beginning teacher conduct a self-evaluation at the midpoint and the end of the school year as a means to evaluate his or her first efforts as a professional educator. The authors provide the reader with a basic instrument that can be used by most teachers.

Materials or Resources

***Form 1.13 Self-Evaluation Instrument
for the Special Education Teacher***

STRATEGY 3: LOCATE A MENTOR TEACHER

A mentor teacher is an individual who can provide the beginning teacher with the emotional support that is helpful as he or she navigates through unfamiliar territory during the first year. Mentor teachers can assist beginning teachers by supplying them with valuable information pertaining to the nuts and bolts of the school's day-to-day operation, serving as role models, sharing knowledge and skills, providing support and encouragement, and, most important, listening. Daugherty (2003) reported in his survey of teachers who had been awarded the Sallie Mae Award, which is given by the American Association of School Administrators and the Student Loan Marketing Association to first-year teachers who have demonstrated superior instructional skills and exhibited excellent interaction with students, faculty, and parents, that "a majority of award winners emphasized the value of mentorship programs aimed at easing the transition from student or intern teacher to professional" (p. 460). Others have discovered that "beginning special education teachers should have weekly contact with their mentors for mentoring to be effective. Also, the mentor optimally would be a special educatory working in the same field and in the same building as the beginning teacher" (Fore, Martin, & Bender, 2002, para. 20). The authors suggest that the new teacher find a mentor who is currently teaching in the same field and building to maximize the effectiveness of the mentoring program.

STRATEGY 4: IDENTIFY ESSENTIAL TASKS

Beginning special education teachers should identify and prioritize all essential tasks that must be accomplished during the pre- and post-planning time periods and on a monthly basis throughout the school year. The authors have developed checklists of items for each period that will help the new teacher establish good work habits and time management skills and successfully complete his or her first year. The authors are aware that a tremendous amount of diversity exists among special education programs and delivery models; despite this fact, however, there continue to be certain tasks that must be accomplished by the teacher of students with exceptionalities if the goal of a successful school year is to be achieved. The contents of every teacher checklist are broken down into four major categories:

- Special education administrative tasks
- General classroom and instructional tasks

- Noninstructional tasks
- Professional learning tasks

The authors recommend that the teacher review each checklist and select the tasks that are relevant and add additional tasks as needed to meet the individual needs of his or her students or program. The authors have created several forms to support the tasks outlined in the planning checklists.

Materials or Resources

Form 1.2 Preplanning Checklist

Form 1.3 Monthly Planning Checklist

Form 1.4 Postplanning Checklist

Form 1.5 Correspondence Log

Form 1.6 Student Emergency Information

Form 1.7 Noninstructional Classroom Supply Checklist

Form 1.8 Instructional Classroom Supply Checklist

Form 1.9 Classroom Inventory Checklist

Form 1.11 Student Service Information

Form 1.12 Present Levels of Performance

STRATEGY 5: ORIENT ASSIGNED PARAPROFESSIONALS

"Paraprofessionals are non-certified staff members who are employed to assist certified staff in carrying out the education programs and otherwise helping in the instruction of students with disabilities" (Friend & Bursuck, 2002, p. 103). The new teacher typically has the primary responsibility of orienting the paraprofessional assigned to his or her special education program. The teacher should include the following in his or her orientation session: define the individual's role and responsibilities, outline classroom expectations and procedures, discuss the rules of confidentiality, take the paraprofessional on a tour of the school, review the school's faculty handbook, discuss basic school information, and preview the areas in which the paraprofessional will be evaluated at the end of the year. The authors have developed a checklist of the most common responsibilities of paraprofessionals and have included a list of suggestions for working with these individuals (Form 1.10). This information is located in the supplemental forms and resources section of this chapter. The teacher must emphasize that the paraprofessional is an important member of the special education team and plays a critical role in facilitating the education process for students. Paraprofessionals need periodic feedback from the supervising teacher to address areas of concern and provide positive reinforcement for effective practices. Salend (2001) states,

> Feedback can include job performance, rapport with students and other school personnel, and information on how to work more effectively. You can also ask paraeducators and volunteers for their point of view about their roles in the school, and you can acknowledge their contributions with notes from students and teachers, graphs or other records of student progress, certificates of appreciation, and verbal comments. (p. 123)

The teacher will find that his or her assigned paraprofessionals are invaluable assets to both the special and general education classrooms. Often, paraprofessionals who have worked in the same school over a period of time can provide the new teacher with significant information pertaining to the students and the particulars of the school.

Materials or Resources

Form 1.10 Paraprofessional's Classroom Responsibilities Checklist

Resource 1.1 Suggestions for Working With a Paraprofessional

STRATEGY 6: ESTABLISH A COMMUNICATION SYSTEM

The new teacher must establish a system for communicating with parents and students in order to establish rapport and build solid partnerships. The authors recommend the following activities to assist the teacher in his or her efforts to implement an effective communication system:

Conduct an Orientation Session

Orientation sessions provide the new teacher with an opportunity to establish communication with parents and students and can assist with setting the tone for the remainder of the school year. The best time to conduct an orientation session is prior to the start of the new school year. Most schools have an "open house" prior to the start of school, and the new teacher could incorporate his or her orientation into this activity. Teachers can take this opportunity to introduce all staff members who will be working with students, provide parents with a description of the special education program or model, discuss classroom expectations and procedures, preview academic curriculum and materials, and take parents on a tour of the school. The authors recommend that the teacher design a simple needs assessment survey to collect information from parents regarding areas of concern and educational topics of interest that can be addressed through future parent workshops. The teacher should provide an opportunity for parents to evaluate the orientation session to gain insight into the quality of the session and obtain information on areas that need improvement. The evaluation may consist of a pencil-and-paper instrument or a computer-assisted survey.

Conduct Parent Workshops and Information Sessions

Parent workshops and information sessions assist the beginning teacher in building a bridge of understanding and communication with parents. Workshops allow parents to learn new skills and practice others, whereas information sessions provide parents with insight on specific topics of interest or concern. The authors recommend the following steps to plan a quality parent workshop:

Step 1: Select topic or focus

Step 2: Select date, time, and location

Step 3: Develop goals and objectives

Step 4: Collect materials or coordinate to have a guest speaker

Step 5: Develop an agenda

Step 6: Advertise, advertise, and advertise

Step 7: Develop an evaluation instrument

Create an Informative and User-Friendly Web Page

The creation of an informative, user-friendly Web page and e-mail account will maximize the new teacher's ability to disseminate and receive information from parents and students. "Technology can assist in communicating a message which can be received at the convenience of the target audience without the barriers of space, place, or time" (Sabella & Booker, 2003, p. 207). The authors found in their review of school Web sites in the United States that Web pages of teachers differ significantly in design, size, and type of information provided on a page. In light of this discovery, the authors developed three categories of information that they recommend for a teacher's Web page. The reader is cautioned that Web pages are best when kept simple in design and updated on a continuous basis. In addition, the teacher must remember that not every student and parent has access to technology, and critical information should continue to be distributed in a hardcopy format. The authors have included a multitude of Internet links that teachers can use when constructing their pages.

Recommended Web Page Information

Introduction of the special education teacher and staff

a. Teacher and staff pictures (use digital camera)

b. Teacher and staff biographies

c. Teacher and staff telephone numbers with extensions

d. Teacher and staff e-mail addresses

Classroom information

a. Class schedule

b. Classroom policies and procedures

c. Syllabi for academic subjects (possibly by grading period)

d. Weekly homework assignments

e. Highlights of special projects

f. Procedures for requesting a conference with the teacher

Parent and student information and resources

a. Specific grade-level information

b. Monthly class bulletin or newsletter (noting important dates and upcoming events, specific class information, specific academic or social skill of the month, and other tidbits)

c. Web site links

   1. Parent support organizations

   2. Student support organizations

   3. Homework assistance for students

   4. College

   5. Financial aid and scholarships

   6. Career

   7. Career information for specific fields

   8. College entrance exams

Materials or Resources

Resource 1.2 Web Sites for Parents and Students

FORM 1.1   Get to Know Your School Checklist

Directions: The authors suggest that the beginning teacher use the checklist below during the meeting with his or her new principal. The checklist can serve as an agenda for the meeting and assist the teacher in gaining an in-depth understanding of the school and the principal's expectations.

_____ Discuss and review the school's mission or vision statement

_____ Discuss and review the current school improvement plan

    a. Academic program priorities

    b. SIP goals and objectives

    c. Specific school initiatives

_____ School profile

    a. Student demographics

    b. Students on free and reduced lunch (total number only)

    c. Student test data

    d. Student promotion and retention statistics

    e. Student daily average attendance

    f. Student dropout rate

    g. Student graduation statistics

    h. Student diploma completion

    i. Student extracurricular activities and organizations

    j. Student discipline information

    k. Special education programs

_____ Principal's expectations of teachers

    a. Observations

    b. Lesson plans

    c. Parent communication

    d. Classroom management

    e. Extracurricular activities

    f. School committees

    g. School duties

_____ Miscellaneous information

    a. School hours for students and teachers

    b. Faculty meetings dates and times

    c. Yearly school calendar of activities and important dates

    d. Name of assigned mentor

FORM 1.2   Preplanning Checklist

> Purpose: The Preplanning Checklist serves as a guide to ensure that all major tasks have been addressed by the new teacher prior to the start of the new school year. The checklist is divided into five major areas: Special Education Administrative Tasks, Classroom/Instructional Tasks, Noninstructional Tasks, Professional Learning Tasks, and Additional Teacher Tasks.

Special Education Administrative Tasks

_____Procure the name and contact information for the special education person assigned to your school (possibly referred to as the special education coordinator or lead teacher).

_____Procure assigned caseload of students with disabilities from the school's principal, special education director, or special education county/district office.

_____Procure assigned students' Individualized Education Programs (IEPs) from school's principal, special education director, or special education county/district office.

_____Review all students' IEPs and complete Student Service Information Form (Form 1.11).

_____Contact school counselor and review students' schedules for the new school year.

_____Coordinate with the school counselor and place students in general education classes as dictated by the IEP.

_____Conference with teachers of students placed in general education settings.

_____Complete Classroom Adaptations Evaluation form (Form 3.4) and distribute to teachers of students placed in general education settings (see Chapter 3).

_____Distribute necessary student discipline information or addendums to the appropriate school administrator.

_____Create Correspondence Log (Form 1.5) book or other electronic recordkeeping system (e.g., Microsoft Outlook) to document all communications with parents, teachers, school administration, and other important contacts.

_____Complete the Paraprofessional's Classroom Responsibilities Checklist (Form 1.10) and discuss selected tasks with the paraprofessional assigned to your class. Be prepared to clarify and explain all assigned duties.

Classroom/Instructional Tasks

_____Procure and review thoroughly all curriculum guides for subjects the new teacher will be responsible for teaching in general education settings and/or the special education classroom.

_____Review each student's IEP and record important information on the Present Levels of Performance form (Form 1.12).

_____Establish a classroom schedule for academic instruction and specialty/elective courses.

_____Request assistance from the school's technology technician in order to ensure that all technology located in the classroom is in working order:

(Continued)

    a. Teacher computer and password

    b. Student computers and work stations

    c. Electronic whiteboards

    d. InterWrite SchoolPad

    e. LCD projector

    f. Printers

    g. Assistive technology devices for students

_____Procure instructional and supporting materials.

_____Procure lesson plan and grade book. Note: Some school systems use electronic grade book programs. The new teacher should request training if his or her school uses an electronic grade book program.

_____Plan lessons, create units, and organize instructional materials.

_____Post subject area standards and essential questions in highly visible area.

_____Construct bulletin boards that reflect instructional units/themes.

_____Place emergency response and exit procedures in highly visible areas:

    a. Fire drill

    b. Tornado or inclement weather drill

    c. Bomb threat

    d. Lockdown

    e. Other

_____Establish classroom procedures and post in classroom:

    a. Classroom expectations

    b. Grading scale

    c. Class grading procedure

    d. Daily routine/schedule

_____Prepare classroom information packet to be sent home to parents the first day of school (see Chapter 4).

_____Copy Student Emergency Information form (Form 1.6) for the first day of school.

Noninstructional Tasks

_____Procure or request noninstructional supplies. Use the Noninstructional Classroom Supply Checklist (Form 1.7).

_____Inventory the contents of the classroom. Use the Classroom Inventory Checklist (Form 1.9) and record all serial numbers of major equipment and note the condition of all items listed below:

1. Number of student desks
2. Teacher desk
3. Tables
4. Chairs
5. Bookshelves
6. File cabinets
7. Storage cabinets
8. Computer
9. LCD projector
10. Computer table
11. Overhead projector
12. Carts
13. Tape recorders
14. Earphones/headsets
15. Televisions
16. VCR
17. Printer
18. Interactive whiteboard

_____Procure faculty duty roster and note all assigned duties and their dates, times, and locations.

Professional Learning

_____Join at least one professional organization (see Chapter 10).

_____Subscribe to at least one professional periodical (see Chapter 10).

_____Procure a schedule of education conferences and make arrangements to attend at least one conference per school year.

_____Procure a schedule of professional learning opportunities for certified personnel offered through the school system.

_____Start current special education articles notebook.

_____Obtain liability insurance for educators through a professional organization.

Additional Teacher Tasks

_____

_____

_____

_____

_____

_____

_____

_____

_____

_____

_____

FORM 1.3   Monthly Planning Checklist

Special Education Administrative Tasks

_____Review students' current individualized education programs (IEPs).

_____Conduct formative assessments to progress monitor all short-term objectives on students' current IEPs.

_____Annotate all mastered short-term objectives on students' current IEPs.

_____Schedule annual review meetings for students with IEPs expiring within 30 days.

_____Send Student Monitor Information form (Form 3.6b) to teachers of students placed in general education settings (see Chapter 3).

_____Review all monitor results and record information on the Student Monitor Results Summary form (Form 3.7; see Chapter 3).

_____Review students' behaviors plans/contracts and revise where necessary. The authors provide a generic Behavior Contract (Form 4.2) in Chapter 4.

_____Correspond with parents in reference to student progress in the general education classroom.

Classroom/Instructional Tasks

_____Complete instructional plans.

_____Procure materials to support instructional plans.

_____Construct bulletin boards to reflect current instructional units or themes.

_____Prepare progress reports or report cards.

_____Communicate with parents in reference to student progress in the special and general education classroom.

Noninstructional Tasks

_____Check noninstructional supplies and replenish as necessary.

_____Review dates for designated faculty meetings or special education meetings.

Professional Learning Tasks

_____Review professional journals and copy articles of interest and place in a notebook for future reference.

_____Select and read a book on an educational topic of interest.

_____Attend education conferences and professional learning courses.

Additional Teacher Tasks

_____

_____

_____

_____

_____

_____

_____

_____

_____

_____

_____

_____

_____

_____

_____

_____

_____

_____

_____

_____

_____

_____

_____

_____

_____

FORM 1.4 Postplanning Checklist

Special Education Administrative Tasks

_____Review all students' individualized education programs and ensure each plan is current and complete.

_____Annotate all mastered goals and objectives on each students' individualized education program.

_____All individualized education programs should be in a file folder and placed in a secured location (preferably a locking file cabinet).

_____Follow district/county policy for sending IEP folders of students being promoted to the next grade and changing schools to the new special education teacher (example: moving up from elementary to middle school or moving up from middle to high school).

_____Review each student's progress in all general education settings and note final grade.

_____Inform parents of student's progress in general education classes.

_____Contact school counselor and review students' schedules for the new school year (this is especially important for high school students).

_____Coordinate with the school counselor and place students in general education classes for the new school year as dictated by their individualized education programs.

_____Contact special education coordinator or special education director to obtain final instructions before leaving school for the summer.

Classroom/Instructional Tasks

_____Prepare and complete final grades for all special education classes.

_____Submit final grades as directed by the school's registrar or administration.

_____Organize and store instructional materials.

_____Remove and store all bulletin board materials and posters.

_____Return all materials procured from the school media center or other faculty members.

_____Follow school policy for closing out the school year (most schools will have a written checklist for teachers to follow before leaving for the summer).

Noninstructional Tasks

_____Complete noninstructional supplies form for new school year and place order before leaving for the summer.

_____Inventory classroom contents and note all deficiencies.

_____Complete work orders for broken equipment or classroom deficiencies.

_____Review all serial numbers of major equipment.

_____Unplug all equipment in the room.

_____Cover all computer equipment.

_____Store audio and visual equipment.

_____Submit request for additional major end items.

_____Organize teacher's desk and miscellaneous materials.

_____Clean desks, chairs, and tables.

Professional Learning

_____Register for summer professional learning or college courses for recertification.

_____Attend summer education conferences or seminars.

_____File all conference and article information.

Additional Teacher Tasks

_____

_____

_____

_____

_____

_____

_____

_____

_____

_____

_____

_____

_____

_____

_____

_____

_____

_____

_____

FORM 1.5   Correspondence Log

Teacher:_____   Month/Year:_____

Date:_____

Method: Telephone   Letter   Fax   School Note   E-mail

Corresponded with: Mr. Ms. Mrs._____

In reference to:
_____
_____
_____

Date:_____

Method: Telephone   Letter   Fax   School Note   E-mail

Corresponded with: Mr. Ms. Mrs._____

In reference to:
_____
_____
_____

Date:_____

Method: Telephone   Letter   Fax   School Note   E-mail

Corresponded with: Mr. Ms. Mrs._____

In reference to:
_____
_____
_____
_____
_____

FORM 1.6 Student Emergency Information

Student name: _____

Date of birth: _____   Age: _____   Present grade: _____

Student FTE or identification number: _____

Parent or guardian name: _____

Address: _____

Mailing address: _____

Home e-mail address: _____

Home telephone number: _____

Cellular telephone number: _____

Parent or guardian work location: _____

    Telephone number: _____

    Cellular telephone number: _____

    E-mail address: _____

Emergency contact person: _____

    Telephone number: _____

    Cellular telephone number: _____

    E-mail address: _____

Significant medical issues (explain/describe): _____

_____

Medications: _____

Allergies: _____

Wears glasses or contact lenses: Yes or No

Wears hearing aids: Yes or No _____Left ear _____Right ear _____Both ears

Transportation to school: _____Bus _____Car _____Day care van _____Walk

Transportation from school: _____Bus _____Car _____Day care van _____Walk

FORM 1.7   Noninstructional Classroom Supply Checklist

Teacher: _____   School Year: _____

Class/Program: _____   Room Number: _____

_____ White copy paper (8 ½ × 11)
_____ Colored copy paper (8 ½ × 11)

_____ Green	_____ Gray
_____ Ivory	_____ Pink
_____ Goldenrod	_____ Lavender
_____ Salmon	_____ Tan
_____ Canary	_____ Blue

_____ NCR paper (8 ½ × 11)
     White/yellow 2-part
_____ NCR paper (8 ½ × 11)
     White/yellow/pink 3-part
_____ Computer paper (laser or other)
_____ Notebook paper
     _____ Three-ring 10 ¼ × 8, ruled
     (college or wide rule)
     _____ Wire bound, 11 × 8 ½
_____ Composition book 10 × 8
_____ Primary practice paper
_____ Notebook binders
     _____ Three-ring, 1-inch diameter
     _____ Three-ring, 1 ½ inch diameter
     _____ Three-ring, 2-inch diameter
_____ Legal pads 8 ½ × 11
     _____ Canary
     _____ White
_____ Teacher plan book
_____ Teacher grade book
_____ E-Z teacher grader
_____ Ballpoint pens
     _____ Black ink
     _____ Blue ink
     _____ Red ink
     _____ Green ink
_____ Pencils
     _____ #2 standard

_____ Sentence strips
     (3 × 24)
_____ Chart tablets
_____ Chart stand
_____ Index cards
_____ Adhesive notepads
     _____ 2 × 3
     _____ 3 × 3
     _____ 3 × 5
_____ Manila file folders
     _____ File folder labels
     _____ File guides A–Z letter
_____ Transparency film
     _____ Acetate writing roll
     _____ Single sheet
_____ Report folders
     _____ 3-fasteners
     _____ Double pockets
_____ Construction paper
     _____ 9 × 12 assorted
     _____ 12 ×18 assorted
     _____ 18 × 24 assorted
_____ Art craft paper
_____ Bulletin board items
     _____ Paper
     _____ Letters
     _____ Border
     _____ Stencils
_____ Chalk
     _____ White
     _____ Yellow
     _____ Colored
_____ Crayons
_____ Colored markers
_____ Colored pencils

_____ Red correcting

_____ Primary

_____ Mechanical

_____ Permanent markers

     _____ Black

     _____ Blue

     _____ Green

     _____ Red

_____ Highlighter markers

     _____ Set of six highlighters

     _____ Yellow

     _____ Orange

     _____ Blue

_____ Transparency markers

     _____ Black

     _____ Blue

     _____ Red

     _____ Green

_____ Whiteboard dry erase markers

     _____ Set of 4 colors

     _____ Black

     _____ Blue

_____ Masking tape

_____ Adhesive tape

_____ Tape dispenser

_____ Paper punchers

     _____ 3-hole punch

     _____ 2-hole punch

     _____ Electric

_____ Computer supplies

     _____ USB flash drives

     _____ Recordable compact disc (CD-R)

     _____ Mouse pad

     _____ Disc storage box

     _____ Screen and CD cleaner

     _____ Printer cartridge

        (Black, color, or laser)

     _____ Surge protector, six outlets

_____ Gem clips

     _____ Small

     _____ Large

     _____ Ideal clamps

_____ Felt stamp pad

     _____ Black

     _____ Red

     _____ Blue

     _____ Green

_____ Glue

     _____ White squeeze

     _____ Glue stick

     _____ Rubber cement

     _____ Paste, jar

_____ Rulers

_____ Meter sticks

_____ Scissors and shears

     _____ Teacher shears

     _____ Student scissors

_____ Stapler

        (Electric or manual)

_____ Staple remover

_____ Thumbtacks

_____ Wite-Out

     _____ Quick dry, white

     _____ Multipurpose, white

     _____ Pen & Ink

_____ Paper towels

_____ Facial tissues

_____ Window cleaner or

        other cleaning solution

_____ Disposable latex gloves

_____ Anti-bacterial soap

_____ First aid kit

_____ Storage containers

_____ Storage containers

_____ File cabinet (locking)

     _____ Four drawer

     _____ Two drawer

(Continued)

FORM 1.7 (Continued)

List of additional items to order:

_____   _____

_____   _____

_____   _____

_____   _____

_____   _____

_____   _____

_____   _____

_____   _____

_____   _____

_____   _____

_____   _____

_____   _____

_____   _____

_____   _____

_____   _____

_____   _____

_____   _____

_____   _____

_____   _____

_____   _____

_____   _____

_____   _____

_____   _____

_____   _____

_____   _____

_____   _____

FORM 1.8   Instructional Classroom Supply Checklist

Teacher:_____   School Year:_____

Class/Program:_____   Room Number:_____

_____Curriculum guides and maps for all subject areas

_____Approved textbooks to support curriculum

_____Teacher editions and resource kits for all textbooks

_____Workbooks and other supporting academic materials

_____Large-print materials

_____Books on tape or CD

_____Supplemental reading material

_____Computer programs to support academic areas

_____Visual aids to support academic areas

_____Manipulative and models

_____Technological devices

_____Audio-visual aids

_____Telecommunication systems

_____Additional items:

_____ _____

_____ _____

_____ _____

_____ _____

_____ _____

_____ _____

_____ _____

_____ _____

_____ _____

_____ _____

_____ _____

FORM 1.9   Classroom Inventory Checklist

Teacher: _____   School year: _____

Class: _____   Room number: _____

Item	Quantity	Item Description and Serial Number	Condition of Item

FORM 1.10 Paraprofessional's Classroom Responsibilities Checklist

Teacher's name: _____   School year: _____

Paraprofessional's name: _____   Program: _____

_____Assist students in computer lab

_____Assist students in the cafeteria

_____Assist students in the media center

_____Assist teacher with academic groups

_____Assist students using adaptive equipment or assistive technology devices

_____Assist with the moving of students to different areas or classes

_____Assist students with specific health needs (paraprofessional must be trained by a licensed health care professional to assist with specific tasks such as the suctioning of a tracheotomy tube, etc.)

_____File students' papers

_____Grade students' academic work

_____Laminate instructional materials

_____Maintain behavior point sheets

_____Make copies of instructional materials

_____Monitor students during recess

_____Monitor/assist students arriving on school bus or special van

_____Organize classroom materials

_____Record daily student attendance

_____Tutor students in academic areas

Additional tasks (list):

_____

_____

_____

_____

_____

_____

_____

_____

_____

_____

_____

_____

_____

_____

_____

FORM 1.11 Student Service Information

Teacher: _____

School year: _____

School: _____

Program: _____

Student Name and Student FTE or ID Number	Student Disability	Current Psychological Date	Current Eligibility Date	IEP Start/ End Dates	Hours Served in Special Education	Hours Served in General Education	Medical Concerns and/or Medications	Additional Information

FORM 1.12   Present Level Is of Performance

Teacher: _____

School: _____

School year: _____

Program: _____

Student Name	Word Recognition Level	Reading Comprehension Level	Written Expression Level	Spelling Level	Math Calculation Level	Math Reasoning Level	Adaptive Behavior Level

FORM 1.13   Self-Evaluation Instrument for the Special Education Teacher

PURPOSE: The authors suggest that the beginning teacher conduct a self-evaluation at the midpoint and the end of the school year as a means to evaluate his or her first efforts as a professional educator.

Indicators	Performance Levels		
Professional Learning	Exemplary	Satisfactory	*Needs Improvement*
The special education teacher participates in professional learning activities in order to stay current in his or her field.			
The special education teacher participates in professional learning activities in order to stay current in best instructional practices.			
The special education teacher attends district, state, and/or national conferences on a yearly basis.			
The special education teacher has memberships and participates in professional organizations.			
The special education teacher continuously seeks to develop and maintain his or her technology skills.			
The special education teacher collaborates with colleagues.			
The special education teacher develops and maintains a professional portfolio.			
The special education teacher maintains a journal highlighting both successful and unsuccessful strategies and activities.			
Additional:			

Indicators	Performance Levels		
Professional Responsibilities	Exemplary	Satisfactory	*Needs Improvement*
The special education teacher clearly understands state and federal laws regarding students with disabilities.			
The special education teacher clearly understands the No Child Left Behind Act and his or her state's requirements pertaining to making Adequate Yearly Progress.			
The special education teacher uses formative assessments to progress monitor students' goals and objectives.			

Indicators	Performance Levels		
Professional Responsibilities	Exemplary	Satisfactory	Needs Improvement
The special education teacher uses summative assessments to annotate students' goals and objectives that were achieved during the school year.			
The special education teacher maintains current IEPs for all students and reviews students' individual goals and objectives on a regular basis.			
The special education teacher conducts parent conferences in a professional and timely manner.			
The special education teacher maintains an up-to-date communication log. The log is a record of communication sent and received during the school year.			
The special education teacher conducts needs assessments with parents and students on a yearly basis.			
The special education teacher conducts orientation sessions and workshops with parents and students throughout the school year.			
The special education teacher communicates effectively with general education teachers and other school personnel.			
The special education teacher supervises assigned paraprofessionals effectively.			
The special education teacher meets regularly with assigned paraprofessionals and provides the individuals with the feedback necessary to promote effective practices.			
The special education teacher develops a yearly budget that adequately supports classroom instruction and activities.			
The special education teacher meets annually with feeder school special education teachers to coordinate the transition of students.			
The special education teacher creates and maintains a Web page on the school's Web site.			
The special education teacher utilizes his or her Web page to communicate information to the school community.			

(Continued)

FORM 1.13 (Continued)

Indicators	Performance Levels		
Professional Responsibilities	Exemplary	Satisfactory	*Needs Improvement*
The special education teacher develops a yearly calendar of special classroom events and major school activities (guest speakers, fieldtrips, standardized tests, etc.).			
Additional:			

Indicators	Performance Levels		
Classroom Management	Exemplary	Satisfactory	*Needs Improvement*
The special education teacher ensures that the classroom is comfortable and conducive to learning for all students.			
The special education teacher ensures the classroom furniture and equipment is age-appropriate and meets the needs of students with disabilities.			
The special education teacher ensures the classroom's color scheme is pleasant, conducive to learning, and promotes a positive learning environment.			
The special education teacher ensures the physical arrangement of the classroom provides a safe and barrier-free environment for all students.			

Indicators	Performance Levels		
Classroom Management	Exemplary	Satisfactory	Needs Improvement
The special education teacher ensures that the physical arrangement of the classroom is conducive to learning for all students (organization of instructional areas, seating arrangements, independent work areas, etc.).			
The special education teacher ensures that bulletin boards, posters, and other visual aids promote student learning.			
The special education teacher obtains adaptive equipment and/or assistive technology needed to instruct or assist students (special tables for students in wheelchairs, amplification equipment for hearing-impaired students, Braille note-taker for students with visual impairments, etc.).			
The special education teacher establishes clear classroom expectations and communicates these expectations effectively to students and parents (i.e., appropriate classroom rules and consequences).			
The special education teacher develops and implements effective behavior management strategies.			
The special education teacher establishes appropriate classroom policies pertaining to the following: grading system/method, reporting student progress, and reporting final grades; late academic work, class work, homework, and make-up work; tardiness and absences; and required class materials.			
The special education teacher establishes appropriate classroom procedures pertaining to the following: how students enter and exit the room; excusing students to use the restroom, get water, and use lockers; how and when students can use learning centers, computers, and other classroom equipment; and where students are to place personal items in the classroom.			
The special education teacher develops classroom schedules that include all academic instruction, specialty/elective classes (art, physical education, music, etc.), and/or special services (speech, occupational therapy, etc.).			

(Continued)

FORM 1.13 (Continued)

Indicators	Performance Levels		
Instructional	*Exemplary*	*Satisfactory*	*Needs Improvement*
The special education teacher reviews the IEPs of all students assigned to his or her class before the first day of school and identifies their individual academic goals and objectives that must be addressed during the school year.			
The special education teacher plans for each academic area by completing the following tasks: (a) identifies desired results for each academic area, (b) determines the acceptable evidence of student mastery of identified skills in academic area, (c) plans learning experiences and instruction that are differentiated by design and promote student mastery of identified academic skills.			
The special education teacher reviews and selects instructional materials that are approved and appropriate for assigned students.			
The special education teacher collaborates and plans with any general education teacher with whom he or she is co-teaching.			
The special education teacher differentiates lesson plans in order to meet the needs of all learners.			
The special education teacher prepares a weekly syllabus or homework calendar for students.			
The special education teacher updates his or her Web page weekly and posts all homework assignments and other important class information.			
The special education teacher prepares lessons in advance and obtains all reinforcement materials (makes copies, obtains maps and/or videos, checks technology devices, etc.).			
The special education teacher plans independent academic activities ("sponges") for periods of time preceding major activities/events, transitions, and/or dismissal ("sponges" are activities that assist students in reviewing or practicing skills previously taught in the classroom).			
The special education teacher identifies and posts all instructional standards and essential questions in a highly visible location in the classroom and refers to this information prior to the start of each lesson.			

Indicators	Performance Levels		
Instructional	Exemplary	Satisfactory	*Needs Improvement*
The special education teacher uses an activating strategy prior to the start of each lesson as a means to focus students on the learning.			
The special education teacher assists students in connecting the purpose of the lessons to prior knowledge and their lives.			
The special education teacher gives clear explanations, and relevant and concrete examples of content.			
The special education teacher models new skills and provides students with guided practice opportunities.			
The special education teacher designs and implements activities that promote student engagement (active listening and responding).			
The special education teacher uses manipulatives and models to assist students in understanding the skills or concepts being taught.			
The special education teacher uses questioning techniques that promote critical thinking and/or check the level of students' understanding of content.			
The special education teacher uses positive feedback with students when responding to questions and/or responses.			
The special education teacher provides opportunities for students to practice new skills independently.			
The special education teacher uses appropriate closure techniques at the end of the lesson.			
The special education teacher assigns homework in order to provide students with an opportunity to practice newly acquired skills.			
The special education teacher uses a variety of techniques to evaluate student mastery of the identified objectives of a lesson (formative assessments, summative assessments, projects, presentations, etc.).			
The special education teacher develops and maintains an academic portfolio for each student.			

(Continued)

FORM 1.13 (Continued)

Indicators	Performance Levels		
Instructional	Exemplary	Satisfactory	Needs Improvement
Additional:			

RESOURCE 1.1   Suggestions for Working With a Paraprofessional

NOTE: In the article "Maximize Paraprofessional Services for Students With Learning Disabilities," Nancy French (2002) emphasizes the need for both general and special education teachers to manage all paraprofessionals in a manner that maximizes their services to students with disabilities. The authors recommend the first-year teacher review the suggestions listed below, which were selected from French's original list of twenty, before working with his or her assigned paraprofessional.

1. Provide orientation.

2. Determine your program and student needs.

3. Consult with classroom teachers to determine their needs.

4. Create a personalized job assignment for the teaching assistant.

5. Determine the training needs of the teaching assistant.

6. Teach and coach new skills.

7. Give feedback on the performance of new skills.

8. Observe and coach the paraprofessional.

9. Provide work plans.

10. Hold meetings.

Source: Adapted from French (2002).

RESOURCE 1.2   Web Sites for Parents and Students

I. ORGANIZATIONS AND RESOURCES FOR PARENTS

American Association of People with Disabilities Act
   http://www.aapd.com/

American Foster Care Resources
   http://www.afcr.com/

Autism Society of America
   http://www.autism-society.org/site/PageServer

Children and Adults With Attention Deficit/Hyperactivity Disorder (CHADD)
   http://www.chadd.org/

Council of Independent Colleges
   http://www.cic.edu/

Eric Clearing House on Disabilities and Gifted Education
   http://ericee.org/

Family and Parenting Resource Center
   http://www.learning4liferesources.com

Family Education
   http://www.familyeducation.com

Middle Web
   http://www.middleweb.com

NASP Center: Helping Children Achieve Their Best. In School. At Home. In Life.
   http://www.nasponline.org/families/index.aspx

II. ORGANIZATIONS AND RESOURCES FOR PARENTS

National Association for Gifted Children
   http://www.nagc.org/

National Coalition for Parent Involvement in Education
   http://www.ncpie.org

National Down Syndrome Society
   http://www.ndss.org/

National Military Family Association
   http://www.nmfa.org/

National PTA
   http://www.pta.org

National Stepfamily Resource Center
   http://www.stepfam.org/

NEA: Help for Parents—Parent Involvement in Education
   http://www.nea.org/parents/research-parents.html

NEAG Center for Gifted and Talent Development
   http://www.gifted.uconn.edu/parents/parentws.html

Organizations for Parents of Blind and Physically Handicapped Children

Parents Count: Resources for Parents of Middle School Students
   http://www.parentscount.net/guidance/detail.cfm?articleID=59

Parent Resource Center: At Risk Youth Programs Help for Parents With a Troubled Teen
   http://www.parenthelpcenter.org/

Partnership for a Drug-Free America
> http://www.drugfreeamerica.org/

The Compassionate Friends
> http://www.compassionatefriends.org/

The Families and Advocates Partnership for Education (FAPE)
> http://www.fape.org/

The Council for Exceptional Children
> www.cec.sped.org/home.htm

III. ORGANIZATIONS AND RESOURCES FOR STUDENTS

American Student Achievement Institute 4-Year High School Course Plans
> http://asai.indstate.edu/guidingallkids/4yrhscourseplan.htm

Amputee Resource Foundation of America, Inc.
> http://www.amputeeresource.org/

Bethesda-Chevy Chase High School: Student Support Programs
> http://www.mcps.k12.md.us/schools/bcchs/support.programs.html

Educate Online
> http://www.esylvan.com/

Health Careers—An Internet Resource Guide for High School Students
> http://www.mccg.org/healthcareers/healthcareershome.asp

Health Occupations Students of America
> http://www.hosa.org

Math Help, Homework Help, and Online Tutoring Web Sites
> http://www.homeschoolmath.net/online/math_help_tutoring.php

MiddleWeb's Hot Links
> http://www.middleweb.com/mw/aaHotLinks.html

National FFA Organization
> http://www.ffa.org

Online Spanish Tutorial
> http://www.LearnPlus.com/

Students Against Drunk Driving
> http://www.saddonline.com

Teen Learning Network
> http://www.childadvocate.net

The English Tutor Online Tutoring for High School Students
> http://www.theenglishtutor.com/

United Nations
> http://www.unol.org/

YMCA: Youth Earth Service Corps
> http://www.yesc.org/

IV. GENERAL RESOURCES FOR PARENTS AND STUDENTS

A. College Resource Web Sites

American College Testing
> www.act.org/

(Continued)

American Universities
   www.clas.ufl.edu/CLAS/american-universities.html

Business, Trade, and Technical Schools
   www.rwm.org/rwm

CollegeBoard
   www.collegeboard.org/

College Net
   www.collegenet.com/

Kaplan, Inc.
   http://www.kaplan.com/

Peterson's College Information
   www.petersons.com/

B. Financial Aid Resources

AESmentor
   http://aesmentor.org/

College Is Possible Campaign
   http://www.collegeispossible.org/

Department of Education: Office of Postsecondary Education
   http://www.ed.gov/about/offices/list/ope/index.html

FastWeb
   http://www.fastweb.com/

Financial Aid Need Estimator
   http://www.act.org/fane/index.html

Free Application for Federal Student Aid
   http://fafsa.ed.gov/

The Smart Student Guide to Financial Aid
   http://www.finaid.org/

C. Career Resource Web Sites

AESmentor
   http://aesmentor.org/

America's Career Infonet
   http://www.acinet.org/acinet/

Career Magazine
   http://www.careermag.com/

Career Pathways—American Student Achievement Institute
   http://asai.indstate.edu/guidingallkids/careerpathways.htm

JobSmart
   http://www.jobsmart.org/

Monster Board
   http://www.monster.com/

National Career Development Association
   http://ncda.org

Occupational Outlook Handbook
   http://www.bls.gov/oco/

The Real Game
   http://www.realgame.com

The Wall Street Journal Executive Career Site
   http://www.careerjournal.com/

What Color Is Your Parachute?
   http://www.jobhuntersbible.com/

D. Alcohol and Substance Abuse

Al-Anon/Alateen
   www.al-anon-alateen.org

Safe and Drug-Free Schools Program U.S. Department of Education
   www.ed.gov/offices/OESE/SDFS

Substance Abuse and Mental Health Services Administration
   www.samhsa.gov/

E. Violence Prevention

Blueprints for Violence Prevention
   www.Colorado.EDU/cspv/blueprints

Bullying in Schools
   http://www.ericeece.org/pubs/digest/1997/banks97.html

Preventing and Coping With School Violence
   http://www.washingtonea.org/index.php?option=com_content&view=article&id=483

Early Warning, Timely Response: A Guide to Safe Schools
   http://www.athealth.com/consumer/issues/early_warning.html

National Youth Gang Center
   www.iir.com/nygc

F. Mental Health Resources

Child Abuse Prevention Network
   http://child-abuse.com/

Diagnosis, Research, and Pharmaceutical Information
   http://www.mentalhealth.com

RESOURCE 1.3   Assistive Technology Information

A. Assistive Technology Device:

(1) Assistive technology device:

   (A) In general. The term "assistive technology device" means any item, piece of equipment, or product system, whether acquired commercially off the shelf, modified, or customized, that is used to increase, maintain, or improve functional capabilities of a child with a disability.

   (B) Exception. The term does not include a medical device that is surgically implanted, or the replacement of such device.

B. Assistive Technology Service:

(2) Assistive technology service. The term "assistive technology service" means any service that directly assists a child with a disability in the selection, acquisition, or use of an assistive technology device.

C. Sample Assistive Technology Tools and Resources:

- Alternative format books (e.g., tape, CD)
- Talking calculator
- Tape recorder
- Word processor
- Graphic organizer
- Pencil grips
- Specialty paper
- Assistive listening device
- Tape recorder
- Planners

Source: Adapted from U.S. Department of Education (2004) and Raskind (2006).

Understanding Students With Disabilities

Theories and goals of education don't matter a whit if you do not consider your students to be human beings.

—Lou Ann Walker

Students with disabilities possess unique learning characteristics and bring a spectrum of expectations to the school experience. The planning of a quality academic program to effectively meet the needs of a diverse group of students can be a major challenge for the beginning teacher. Frequently, first-year special education teachers are placed in positions that differ substantially from their training and area of expertise. Mastropieri (2001) found the following in his research on the challenges encountered by first-year special education teachers:

> Some teachers are assigned positions for which they have not been adequately prepared. Sometimes teachers self-select these positions; other times they are assigned such positions. This issue may actually be increasing over time, for several reasons. First, as school districts move toward more inclusive education models, there is an increased expectation for more special education teachers to work with any student with any disability in any setting. Second, as teacher shortages increase, individuals have more options for teaching position available to them. (p. 72)

In addition, the passage of the No Child Left Behind Act presents a set of challenges for teachers in the special education profession. "The cornerstone of the No Child Left Behind Act, signed into law by President Bush on January 8, 2002, is improving results for all students, including those with special needs" (Boehner, 2003, p. 1). The new special education teacher must raise standards and plan programs that result in students meeting adequate yearly progress as outlined in the federal law. The teacher's first step toward meeting most challenges is to obtain a clear understanding of each student's individual needs from an educational, physiological, and emotional perspective. The authors recommend that the new teacher spend a tremendous amount of time prior to the start of the school year in reviewing and analyzing all information pertaining to the students assign to his or her caseload. Next, the teacher should schedule time during the first days of school to meet with students individually in order to begin developing rapport and to obtain students' perceptions of the current special education services. Haraway (2002) states, "we as educators sometimes have difficulty listening, really listening to what students and parents say about what they want, what changes they would like us to consider, and what is working well" (p. 60). Finally, the authors highly recommend that the beginning teacher review the disabilities recognized in the Individuals with Disabilities Education Act (IDEA) in order to have the information necessary to successfully teach in special education delivery models or programs that service students with varying disabilities.

In Chapter 2, the authors present three strategies designed to facilitate the new teacher's quest to understand students with disabilities. The implementation of these strategies will assist the teacher in developing a quality special education program based on student need, in promoting student success in the school setting, and in building a positive rapport between teacher and student. The authors have developed forms and surveys that can assist the teacher as he or she strives to understand students with special needs.

STRATEGY 1: REVIEW STUDENT INFORMATION

The reviewing and analyzing of current student information is a task that is tedious and time consuming; however, this process is typically the initial step prior to designing and implementing a successful educational program for students. All critical information related to each student is usually contained in a confidential file folder that is secured and maintained by the special education teacher. General student information such as attendance and transcripts can be obtained from the student's permanent school record or the school's student information system. The authors have created the Student Folder Checklist and Student Profile (see Forms 2.1 and 2.2) that will guide the new teacher through the review process and the recording of all pertinent student information. All student information is considered highly confidential and may be shared only with individuals who have legal access. The special education teacher should have possession of or access to the following documents for every student on his or her caseload:

- Current individualized education program
- Eligibility document
- Classroom performance (regular and special class)
- Classroom observations
- School discipline information
- School attendance information
- Student transition plan

- Vision and hearing screening results
- Student transportation information
- Student medical information

Materials or Resources:

Form 2.1 Student Folder Checklist

Form 2.2 Student Profile

STRATEGY 2: CONDUCT STUDENT SURVEYS AND INVENTORIES

The first-year special education teacher can use a multitude of strategies in order to obtain a more comprehensive perspective of each student on his or her caseload. The authors recommend that the teacher use student surveys and inventories as a means of obtaining information and gaining insight into how each student processes information in the academic environment and his or her preferred learning style. These instruments are subjective by design and usually provide the student with the opportunity to communicate to the special education teacher his or her personal thoughts, feelings, and opinions in terms of educational needs. In this section, the authors provide the new teacher with simple surveys and inventories designed to extract essential student information. These instruments make for good independent student activities during the first days of school. The teacher must remember that all collected information must be considered confidential and may only be shared with individuals with approved access.

Materials and Resources:

Form 2.3 Student Academic Inventory

The special education teacher completes the inventory once he or she has reviewed all the student information referred to in Strategy 1 of this chapter. The instructor can use this form when developing classroom modifications for students in inclusive settings.

Form 2.4 Student Learning Styles Survey

The survey is to be completed by the student on an independent basis. However, students who are nonreaders may have assistance with completing the form from a teacher or peer. The results of the survey will provide the teacher with information regarding the student's preferred learning style.

Form 2.5 Student Interest Survey

The survey is to be completed by the student on an independent basis. However, students who are nonreaders may have assistance with completing the form from a teacher or peer. The results of the survey will provide the teacher with a greater understanding of the student's personal and school interest.

STRATEGY 3: REVIEW RECOGNIZED DISABILITIES IN IDEA

Special education is constantly evolving and changing in both philosophies and practices as a result of the tremendous amount of research conducted in the field every year. Therefore, it is imperative that teachers be current in the field in their respective areas of expertise. The most prominent changes in practices are the movements toward inclusion of students in the general education classroom and the use of the cross-categorical or interrelated special education classrooms. Typically in the inclusion model, students are placed in regular education classes on a full-time basis with a special education teacher providing services to the student in this setting. Often the special education teacher will team teach with the general education teacher, and other times the special teacher will serve as a consultant to these educators. The primary focus of inclusion is the providing of services to students with disabilities in the least restrictive environment. The cross-categorical or interrelated special education classrooms are designed to serve students with different disabilities but similar levels of severity for academic instruction or support. As a result of these current trends, the authors recommend that beginning teachers review current information on all recognized disabilities prior to the start of school and continue throughout the entire year in order to meet the needs of a diverse group of students with disabilities. In the following pages, the authors provide the reader with the legal definitions for all disabilities that are currently recognized in the regulations of the Individuals with Disabilities Education Act. The authors strongly suggest that readers refer to their state department of education's definitions for disability categories. In addition, supplemental information is provided for the disabilities that the new special education teacher will most likely encounter. All information is presented in an abbreviated format and intended only as a quick review or reference and not as an in-depth study. The authors recommend updating the information provided on a yearly basis.

RECOGNIZED DISABILITIES—SECTION 300.7—CHILD WITH A DISABILITY.

AUTISM

Legally Defined:

Autism means a developmental disability significantly affecting verbal and nonverbal communication and social interaction, generally evident before age three, that adversely affects a child's educational performance. Other characteristics often associated with autism are engagement in repetitive activities and stereotyped movements, resistance to environmental change or change in daily routines, and unusual responses to sensory experiences. (*IDEA '97 Final Regulations*, n.d.)

Typically Required Eligibility Information:

- Psychological evaluation
- Educational evaluation
- Communication evaluation
- Behavioral observations
- Developmental history

DEAF-BLINDNESS

Legally Defined:

Deaf-blindness means concomitant hearing and visual impairments, the combination of which causes such severe communication and other developmental and educational needs that they cannot be accommodated in special education programs solely for children with deafness or children with blindness. (*IDEA '97 Final Regulations*, n.d.)

Typically Required Eligibility Information:

- Audiological evaluation
- Otological evaluation
- Ophthalmological evaluation

DEAFNESS

Legally Defined:

Deafness means a hearing impairment that is so severe that the child is impaired in processing linguistic information through hearing, with or without amplification, that adversely affects a child's educational performance. (*IDEA '97 Final Regulations*, n.d.)

Typically Required Eligibility Information:

- Otological evaluation
- Audiological evaluation

EMOTIONAL DISTURBANCE

Legally Defined:

(i) The term means a condition exhibiting one or more of the following characteristics over a long period of time and to a marked degree that adversely affects a child's educational performance:

   (A) An inability to learn that cannot be explained by intellectual, sensory, or health factors.

    (B) An inability to build or maintain satisfactory interpersonal relationships with peers and teachers.

    (C) Inappropriate types of behavior or feelings under normal circumstances.

    (D) A general pervasive mood of unhappiness or depression.

    (E) A tendency to develop physical symptoms or fears associated with personal or school problems.

  (ii) The term includes schizophrenia. The term does not apply to children who are socially maladjusted, unless it is determined that they have an emotional disturbance under paragraph (c)(4)(i) of this section. (*IDEA '97 Final Regulations,* n.d.)

Typically Required Eligibility Information:

- Psychological evaluation
- Educational evaluation
- Behavioral observations
- Social history

HEARING IMPAIRMENT

Legally Defined:

Hearing impairment means an impairment in hearing, whether permanent or fluctuating, that adversely affects a child's educational performance but that is not included under the definition of deafness in this section. (*IDEA '97 Final Regulations,* n.d.)

Types of Hearing Loss:

1. Conductive hearing losses are due to blockage or damage to the outer or middle ear that prevents sound waves from traveling (being conducted) to the inner ear. Generally, someone with a conductive hearing loss has a mild to moderate disability. Some conductive hearing losses are temporary.

2. Sensorineural hearing loss occurs when there is damage to the inner ear or the auditory nerve (the eighth cranial nerve), and usually cannot be improved medically or surgically. Individuals affected by a sensorineural loss are able to hear different frequencies at different intensity levels; their hearing losses are not flat or even. Sensorineural losses are less common in young children than the conductive types (Smith & Luckasson, 1992, p. 385).

3. Congenital hearing losses occur during fetal development or during birth. Most congenital hearing losses are sensorineural and due to either genetic defects or nongenetic factors such as rubella, diabetes, or an underactive thyroid in the mother during pregnancy (Gearheart, Mullen, & Gearheart, 1993, pp. 234–235).

Assistive Listening Devices for Students With Hearing Impairments:

- Hearing aids
- Auditory trainers
- Audio loop

Typically Required Eligibility Information:

- Audiological evaluation
- Otological evaluation
- Educational evaluation

Table 2.1 Levels of Hearing Impairment

Hearing Thresholds	Ability to Understand Speech
26–40 dB	Difficulty only with faint speech
41–70 dB	Frequent difficulty with normal speech
71–90 dB	Can understand only shouted or amplified speech
91 dB or more	Usually can't hear any speech

Source: Schildroth and Karchmer (1986, p. 12).

MENTAL RETARDATION

Legally Defined:

Mental retardation means significantly subaverage general intellectual functioning, existing concurrently with deficits in adaptive behavior and manifested during the developmental period, that adversely affects a child's educational performance. (*IDEA '97 Final Regulations,* n.d.)

Etiology:

On the basis of current knowledge, approximately 25 percent of all cases of mental retardation are known to be caused by biological abnormalities. Chromosomal and metabolic disorders—such as Down syndrome, fragile X syndrome, and phenylketonuria (PKU)—are the most common disorders manifesting mental retardation. Mental retardation associated with these disorders is usually diagnosed at birth or relatively early in childhood, and the severity is generally moderate to profound.

No specific biological causes can be identified in the remaining 75 percent of the cases. The level of intellectual impairment of a person with no known cause is usually mild, with an I.Q. between 50 to 70. The diagnosis of mild retardation is not usually made before grade school. In mild mental retardation, a familial pattern is often seen in parents and siblings. (Kaplan, Sadock, & Grebb, 1991, p. 686)

Prenatal Factors

Rubella (German measles)

Cytomegalic inclusion diseases

Syphilis

AIDS

Complications of pregnancy

Substance abuse

Chromosomal Abnormalities

Down syndrome

Cat-cry (cri-du-chat) syndrome

Fragile X syndrome

Rett's syndrome

Genetic Factors

Phenylketonuria (PKU)

Menkes's disease

Hartnup disease

Galactosemia

Glycogen storage disease

Acquired Childhood Conditions

Infection: Encephalitis and meningitis

Head trauma

Other issues: cardiac arrest, asphyxia, chronic exposure to lead, and chemotherapy

Typically Required Eligibility Information:

- Psychological evaluation
- Educational evaluation
- Adaptive behavior evaluation
- Relevant medical information

MULTIPLE DISABILITIES

Legally Defined:

Multiple disabilities means concomitant impairments (such as mental retardation-blindness, mental retardation-orthopedic impairment, etc.), the combination of which causes such severe educational needs that they cannot be accommodated in the special education programs solely for one of the impairments. The term does not include deaf-blindness. (*IDEA '97 Final Regulations*, n.d.)

ORTHOPEDIC IMPAIRMENT

Legally Defined:

Orthopedic impairment means a severe orthopedic impairment that adversely affects a child's educational performance. The term includes impairments caused by congenital anomaly, . . . impairments caused by disease (e.g., poliomyelitis, bone tuberculosis, etc.), and impairments from other causes (e.g., cerebral palsy, amputations, and fractures or burns that cause contractures). (*IDEA '97 Final Regulations*, n.d.)

Typically Required Eligibility Information:

- Medical examination
- Educational evaluation
- Psychological evaluation

OTHER HEALTH IMPAIRMENT

Legally Defined:

Other health impairment means having limited strength, vitality or alertness, including a heightened alertness to environmental stimuli, that results in limited alertness with respect to the educational environment, that—

(i) Is due to chronic or acute health problems such as asthma, attention deficit disorder or attention deficit hyperactivity disorder, diabetes, epilepsy, a heart condition, hemophilia, lead poisoning, leukemia, nephritis, rheumatic fever, and sickle cell anemia; and

(ii) Adversely affects a child's educational performance. (*IDEA '97 Final Regulations*, n.d.)

Typically Required Eligibility Information:

- Medical examination
- Educational evaluation
- Psychological evaluation

SPECIFIC LEARNING DISABILITY

Legally Defined:

(i) *General.* The term means a disorder in one or more of the basic psychological processes involved in understanding or in using language, spoken or written, that may manifest itself in an imperfect ability to listen, think, speak, read, write, spell, or to do mathematical calculations, including such conditions as perceptual disabilities, brain injury, minimal brain dysfunction, dyslexia, and developmental aphasia.

(ii) *Disorders not included.* The term does not include learning problems that are primarily the result of visual, hearing, or motor disabilities, of mental retardation, of emotional disturbance, or of environmental, cultural, or economic disadvantage. (*IDEA '97 Final Regulations*, n.d.)

General Information:

The authors can find no nationally consistent method for determining whether a student has a specific learning disability (SLD). The use of discrepancy scores and formulas is one of the most common approaches for identifying students with specific learning disabilities. In this approach, a standardized intelligence test and standardized achievement test are administered to the student. The results from the intelligence test reveal the student's potential while the achievement test results demonstrate the student's actual academic performance. The student's standard scores on both tests are reviewed and evaluated for significant discrepancies. The following is a list of characteristics of the SLD student:

Mixed Dominance	*LD in Family*
Directional confusion	Sequencing problems
No concept of time	Retrieval difficulty
Attention problems	Poor motor control
Disorganized	Reversals
Poor oral reading	Inability to copy
Poor spelling	Trouble with written expression
Leaky memory	Problem with attitude, motivation, and behavior
Creative	

Typically Required Eligibility Information:

- Psychological evaluation
- Comprehensive educational evaluation
- Analyzed samples of work
- Classroom observation
- Relevant medical information

SPEECH OR LANGUAGE IMPAIRMENT

Legally Defined:

Speech or language impairment means a communication disorder, such as stuttering, impaired articulation, a language impairment, or a voice impairment, that adversely affects a child's educational performance. (*IDEA '97 Final Regulations*, n.d.)

General Information:

Speech disorders: voice, articulation, and fluency

Language disorders: form (phonology, morphology, and syntax), content (semantics), and use (pragmatics)

Typically Required Eligibility Information:

- Oral peripheral examination
- Articulation evaluation
- Language evaluation
- Voice evaluation
- Fluency

TRAUMATIC BRAIN INJURY

Legally Defined:

Traumatic brain injury means an acquired injury to the brain caused by an external physical force, resulting in total or partial functional disability or psychosocial impairment, or both, that adversely affects a child's educational performance. The term applies to open or closed head injuries resulting in impairments in one or more areas, such as cognition; language; memory; attention; reasoning; abstract thinking; judgment; problem-solving; sensory, perceptual, and motor abilities; psychosocial behavior; physical functions; information processing; and speech. The term docs not apply to brain injuries that are congenital or degenerative, or to brain injuries induced by birth trauma. (*IDEA '97 Final Regulations*, n.d.)

Typically Required Eligibility Information:

- A formal report of pre-injury functioning
- Medical report
- Psychological evaluation

VISUAL IMPAIRMENT

Legally Defined:

Visual impairment including blindness means an impairment in vision that, even with correction, adversely affects a child's educational performance. The term includes both partial sight and blindness. (*IDEA '97 Final Regulations*, n.d.)

Typically Required Eligibility Information

- Ophthalmologic evaluation
- Educational evaluation

FORM 2.1   Student Folder Checklist

Directions: The teacher should complete the Student Folder Checklist form while simultaneously reviewing each IEP folder in his or her possession. All questions and concerns in reference to the reviewed student information must be noted at the bottom of the form. All information contained on this form is considered highly confidential.

Student Name:_____   Date:_____

Student Disability:_____   Grade:_____

Information	Yes	No	Comments
Individualized education plan (current IEP)			
Eligibility document			
Classroom performance			
Classroom observation			
School discipline information			
School attendance information			
Student transition plan			
Vision and hearing screening results			
Transportation information			
Medical information			
Miscellaneous information (List): - - - - - - -			

FORM 2.2   Student Profile

Directions: The special education teacher should complete the *Student Profile* form while simultaneously reviewing each student's IEP information.

School Year: _____

Student Name: _____   Date: _____

Disability: _____   Age: _____   Grade: _____

Student's academic strengths:

_____

_____

_____

_____

_____

_____

_____

Student's academic challenges:

_____

_____

_____

_____

_____

_____

Student's behavior or emotional challenges:

_____

_____

_____

_____

_____

_____

(Continued)

FORM 2.2 (Continued)

Student's adaptive behavior issues:

_____

_____

_____

_____

_____

Student's transition issues:

_____

_____

_____

_____

_____

Additional information:

_____

_____

_____

_____

_____

_____

_____

_____

_____

_____

_____

_____

_____

_____

FORM 2.3 Student Academic Inventory

Directions: The special education teacher should complete a *Student Academic Inventory* upon reviewing each student's current IEP, assessments (formal and informal), and classroom performance information.

Student Name: _____   Date: _____

Current Grade: _____   Age: _____   Disability: _____

How the Student Learns

Sources from which the student can best receive, process, and retrieve academic information	Strengths	Challenges	Instructional Delivery Method	Strengths	Challenges
Textbook			Direct		
Worksheets			Independent study		
Lecture			Peer tutor		
Class discussions			1–1 teacher assistance		
Audio-visual material			Small group		
Hands-on experiences			Large group		
Observation			Computer-managed		
Other:(List)			Other: (List)		

How the Student Responds

Academic testing formats that the student can best demonstrate his or her degree of skill mastery	Strengths	Challenges	Academic Course Assignments	Strengths	Challenges
Written test			Short papers		
Oral test			Worksheets		
Short answer test			Oral reports		
Essay test			Textbook exercises		
Multiple-choice test			Course projects		
True-false test			Presentations		
Matching test			Vocabulary exercises		
Computation test			Science labs		
Other: (List)			Other: (List)		

FORM 2.4   Student Learning Styles Survey

Directions: The *Student Learning Styles Survey* is designed to help your teachers in planning and implementing effective instructional programs. Please answer the questions below to the best of your ability to help the teacher in to get a true understanding of your learning style.

Student Name: _____   Date: _____

Class: _____   Grade: _____

1. What kinds of tests do you like best?
    _____True/false
    _____Fill-in-the-blank
    _____Multiple choice
    _____Discussion
    _____Matching
    _____Other (list) _____

2. When is it the hardest to take notes?
    _____During class lectures
    _____From the chalkboard
    _____From the overhead projector
    _____Other (what kind) _____

3. When is learning easiest?
    _____Reading material by myself
    _____Class lecture
    _____Working with a peer
    _____Listening to material on tape
    _____Other (list/explain) _____

4. Where do you like to study?
    _____In my bedroom
    _____A quiet place
    _____A place with music
    _____In the library
    _____Other (list/explain) _____

5. When do you study best?
    _____Morning
    _____Afternoon
    _____Night

6. What school subject is the hardest for you?
    _____Reading _____English _____Writing
    _____Math _____Science _____Social studies
    _____Other (list) _____

Check		Comments
	I can read tests given in class to myself.	
	I can take notes in class without help.	
	I can read class textbooks out loud or to myself.	
	I understand the content in my class textbooks.	
	I can communicate with my teachers.	
	Class material is easier for me to understand when we do labs or other hands-on activities.	
	I write in an assignment book every day.	
	I am organized for each class every day.	
	I have a set study time or schedule and location.	
	I study for tests and quizzes in advance.	

Student Comments:

_____

_____

_____

_____

_____

_____

_____

_____

_____

_____

_____

_____

_____

_____

_____

_____

_____

_____

FORM 2.5   Student Interest Survey

Directions: The purpose of the *Student Interest Survey* is to help your teacher get to know you. Please answer all the questions listed in the survey. A teacher, parent, or friend can read the survey to you and assist with the recording of your responses on the form.

Student Name: _____   Date: _____

1. I like to read about _____

_____

2. In my free time I like _____

_____

3. I like people _____

_____

4. My favorite author is _____

_____

5. When I grow up I want to be _____

_____

6. My favorite subject in school is _____

_____

7. My hobby/hobbies are _____

_____

8. I don't like books that _____

_____

9. The place I would like to visit most is _____

_____

10. My favorite vacation was _____

_____

11. The thing I like to do most is _____

_____

12. What I want most in the world is_____

_____

13. I wish _____

_____

14. My favorite song is _____

_____

15. My favorite book is _____

_____

16. My favorite color is _____

_____

17. My favorite food is _____

_____

18. My favorite movie is _____

_____

19. My favorite sport is _____

_____

20. This school year I will _____

_____

Additional Information:

_____

_____

_____

_____

_____

_____

_____

Placing Students in the Least Restrictive Environment

The dream begins, most of the time, with a teacher who believes in you, who tugs and pushes and leads you on to the next plateau, sometimes poking you with a sharp stick called truth.

—Dan Rather

The term *least restrictive environment* refers to the educational setting for students with disabilities that provides the greatest exposure to the general education curriculum and to an interaction with nondisabled students. The Individuals with Disabilities Education Act rules and regulations (Section 300.114) mandate that the IEP (individualized education program) team make every effort to ensure that students with disabilities are placed with nondisabled students to the maximum extent possible and that removal from this environment is the last resort. Placement of students with disabilities begins with the development of the initial IEP after a student is determined eligible for services. Thereafter, the team must address the issue of placement in the least restrictive environment on a yearly basis. During the past several years the placement of students with disabilities has become an issue that has grown to be a major concern for both special and general education teachers throughout the nation primarily due to the passage of the No Child Left Behind (NCLB) act. The specific performance expectations and adequate yearly progress provision in NCLB pertain to all students and have placed a tremendous amount of pressure on school systems to ensure that students with disabilities are progressing at the same rate as nondisabled students. In light of NCLB, school systems are encouraging the placement of students with disabilities into general education classrooms on a full-time basis with special education teachers delivering services to these students through an inclusion or collaborative model. The beginning teacher must remember that there is a continuum of service delivery options for students with disabilities ranging from the least restrictive environment (general classroom on a full-time basis) to the most restrictive environment (hospitals and institutions), and the IEP team must determine the educational environment that best meets the needs of the student.

In the pages that follow, the authors provide the beginning teacher with the information, suggestions, and strategies that are critical to placing students with disabilities in the least restrictive environment. The chapter is divided into six sections, with each section targeting some aspect of the placement process. The chapter begins with the authors' review of three service delivery models that the beginning teacher is most likely to encounter during his or her first teaching experience and explains the advantages and disadvantages of each model. The authors continue in the chapter with the outlining of specific student information for the IEP team to review before making their final placement decision and provide the IEP team with a selection of general classroom modifications and strategies that can be used for students with disabilities in most educational settings. The authors have designed checklists, surveys, supplemental forms, and helpful hints to assist and support the special education teacher and IEP team.

SECTION 1: REVIEW OF SERVICE DELIVERY MODELS

Students with disabilities can receive special education services in a variety of educational settings that range from the general education classroom to a residential care facility. The IEP team determines the most appropriate placement for the student based on his or her educational needs and must document all placement options considered and rejected by the team. The information that follows is an overview of three special education service delivery models that the beginning teacher will most likely encounter in his or her new position.

General Class Full-Time

In this delivery model, which is often referred to as inclusion or collaborative, the student is placed and receives instruction in a general education classroom for most or all of the school day. Typically, students only leave the classroom to receive a related service such as speech therapy, counseling, or other service as required by the student's IEP. In the inclusion or collaborative model, the special education teacher can use several methods to provide services to the student. The special education teacher can directly serve the student in the general education classroom or consult, team, or co-teach with the general education teacher. The key to the successful placement of students with disabilities in the general education environment is collaboration, communication, and prior planning.

Advantages:

1. Students gain the benefits of being fully included with their peers.

2. Students receive one-on-one or small group instruction geared to their individual learning needs.

3. All students and teachers learn about diversity and accommodating to individual needs.

Disadvantages:

1. Some teachers find it difficult to have another teacher in their classrooms.

2. Scheduling time to meet with children in many classes can be difficult.

3. Some children need more support than short visits from the special education teacher can provide.

4. Most teachers do not have enough time to effectively teach to all the needs in the classroom. (Bureau of Jewish Education, 2006, p. 9)

Special Class Part-Time or Pullout Program

The student is placed and receives instruction in a special education classroom for part of the school day. In this model, which is often referred to as resource or a pullout program, the special education teacher instructs the student in a small group or on an individual basis in the areas of identified need. The student is usually mainstreamed for the remainder of the school day into general education classrooms and/or activities as deemed appropriated by the IEP team. Mainstreaming is the placing of students with disabilities in an educational environment with students that do not have disabilities for a designated period of time during the regular school day. The placement can be of an academic, nonacademic, or extracurricular nature. The special education teacher provides the regular education teacher with the necessary modifications for the student to be successful in his or her mainstreamed classes.

Advantages:

1. Students gain the social benefits of being with their peers in a mainstream class.

2. Students receive one-on-one or small group instruction geared to their individual learning needs.

3. All students and teachers learn about diversity and accommodating to individual needs.

Disadvantages:

1. Students sometimes miss interesting or important lessons when they are pulled out.

2. Students may feel stigmatized by being pulled out.

3. Scheduling can be difficult.

4. Sometimes students cannot keep up with the work of the mainstream class. (Bureau of Jewish Education, 2006, p. 8)

Special Class Full-Time

Students receive their primary instruction in the special education classroom on a full-time basis. Students in this type of placement are usually mainstreamed into nonacademic classes with nondisabled students.

Advantages:

1. Small class size.

2. Students get curriculum tailored exactly to their needs.

3. Students spend most of their time with a trained special education teacher.

4. Students who cannot succeed in a mainstream class may do well in this setting.

Disadvantages:

1. Students can be isolated from the rest of the school.

2. Student may feel stigmatized by being in a "special class."

3. Students do not get the social benefits of being included with their peers.

4. It is expensive to have one teacher for a small number of students. (Bureau of Jewish Education, 2006, p. 7)

SECTION 2: THE PLACEMENT DECISION

The IEP team must thoroughly review and discuss all current information pertaining to the student before making their final placement decision. The special education teacher should collect and organize the following student information prior to the IEP meeting:

- School attendance information
- Discipline information
- Current levels of academic performance
- Current status of medical condition (if applicable)
- Classroom observation information
- General education teacher summary report or reports

Once a consensus has been reached in terms of the best placement for the student, the IEP team must annotate other placements considered and rejected in the minutes.

Materials and Resources:

Form 3.1 Selecting the Least Restrictive Environment Checklist

Form 3.2 Teacher Summary Report

SECTION 3: CLASSROOM ACCOMMODATIONS AND MODIFICATIONS

The development of appropriate classroom accommodations and/or modifications is critical when placing students in inclusive settings. The team must design or select strategies based on the student's identified deficit or deficits and that will allow the student to progress in the general curriculum. A copy of the agreed-upon classroom accommodations and/or modifications must be given to all teachers who will be working with the student, prior to the student's first day. The authors have included a selection of classroom strategies at the end of this chapter. The special education teacher can attach this information to the student's classroom strategies and distribute to the appropriate teachers.

Materials and Resources:

Form 3.3 Classroom Adaptations

Form 3.4 Classroom Adaptations Evaluation

Form 3.5 Student's Materials List

Resource 3.1 Defining Accommodations and Modifications

SECTION 4: MONITORING STUDENTS IN THE GENERAL EDUCATION SETTING

The special education teacher in some fashion must monitor all students placed in general education settings in order to address academic, behavior, or other problems before they escalate and affect educational performance. The authors have developed four forms that will assist the first-year teacher with the documentation and tracking of student progress.

Materials and Resources:

Form 3.6A Teacher Directions for Completing Student Monitor Form

Form 3.6B Student Monitor Information

Form 3.7 Student Monitor Results Summary

Form 3.8 Individual Student Progress Report Summary

Form 3.9 Individual Student Final Grade Summary

SECTION 5: TIPS FOR THE GENERAL EDUCATION TEACHER

The authors have selected six disabilities recognized in the current regulations of the Individuals with Disabilities Education Act (IDEA) and provide recommended educational strategies for each disability. Both special and general education teachers can use the strategies listed in this section.

Tips for Teachers of Students With Specific Learning Disabilities

1. The student should sit in a location that is free from distractions and in close proximity to the instructor.

2. Write all homework or class assignments on the board.

3. Use peer tutoring or peer helping. The peer tutor or helper can assist the student in the following manner:

   a. Making certain the student understands directions of assignments.
   b. Reading important directions and essential material to the student.
   c. Drilling the student orally on what he or she needs to know.
   d. Orally summarizing important textbook passages for the student.
   e. Working with the student in joint assignments.
   f. Critiquing the student's work and making suggestions for improvement.

4. Use a multisensory approach to instruction when possible.

5. Conference with the student as much as possible in order to verify that the student understands the course material and all instructions.

6. Give the student several alternatives for obtaining and reporting information: tapes, interviews, reading, experience, making something, and the like.

7. Give the student shortened assignments.

8. Set up a specific homework schedule and/or test schedule so the student will know what to expect.

9. Allow the student to underline or highlight in his or her textbook.

10. Encourage the student to utilize flashcards for vocabulary word review.

11. Give positive reinforcement as often as possible.

12. Modify tests or quizzes according to the student's IEP.

Tips for Teachers of Students With Behavioral Disorders

1. Establish clear rules for the class and post in highly visible location.

2. Speech Rules are most effective when they are:

   a. Few in number.
   b. Relatively short.
   c. Stated positively (e.g., "Work quietly" rather than "Do not make noise").
   d. Regularly reviewed with students. (Rizzo & Zabel, 1988, p. 220)

3. Reinforce individual students when they follow the rules.

4. Ignore inappropriate behavior when possible.

5. Ensure that the consequences for not following the rules are fair, realistic, and appropriate for the offense.

6. Develop a "safe plan" for times when the student feels as though he or she is about to lose control (e.g., may go to see the school counselor or stand in the hallway).

7. Provide an environment that is structured.

8. Post the class schedule or routine. The teacher should inform the student in advance of changes to the class schedule.

9. Contact the student's parents to report both positive and negative information—equally.

10. Maintain accurate records on classroom behavior. Contact parents if the student exhibits significant and drastic changes in behavior.

11. Praise the student often.

12. Assign the student room responsibilities that will promote self-confidence.

Tips for Teachers of Other Health Impaired Students

1. Be alert to signs of fatigue in the child.

2. Find teaching materials that can be adapted to the physical needs of the student.

3. Use teaching materials and activities that are appropriate for the age of the student.

4. Make sure that all areas of the room and school are accessible.

5. Make sure materials, projects, or leisure activities are within the student's reach.

6. Encourage personal privacy when assisting the student with hygiene.

7. Include activities each day that the student can accomplish from a wheelchair.

8. Lift only as much weight as you can.

9. Post emergency instructions and telephone numbers. (Smith & Luckasson, 1992, p. 452)

Tips for Teachers of Students With ADD or ADHD

1. Preferential seating: the teacher should design a seating chart that will place the ADD/ADHD/ADIID student in close proximity to instruction and away from areas of distraction.

2. Classroom rules and consequences should be clear and concise and placed in a highly visible area.

3. Present clear, specific, and simple directions in both written and oral form.

4. Post the classroom schedule or routine.

5. Avoid heavy doses of seatwork.

6. Provide an area in the room where the student can retreat when he or she is having a difficult time staying focused or controlling his or her activity level. Study carrels work great for elementary students.

7. Provide the student with concrete activities and examples to demonstrate abstract concepts. Utilize hands-on activities and/or manipulative when possible.

8. Utilize visual and verbal prompts and cues to maintain on-task behavior.

9. Provide the student with opportunities to move around the room—running errands, helping in the classroom, handing out papers, cleaning the board, and so on.

10. Give positive reinforcement for appropriate behavior—immediately.

11. Provide the student with a particular time frame for assignment completion. Assignments should be broken down into smaller pieces. Allow extended amount of time for assignment completion.

12. Use medium intensity lighting.

Tips for Teachers of Students With Hearing Impairments

(Mild to Moderate Hearing Losses)

1. Talk facing the student.

2. The student should sit close to the teacher or direction of instruction.

3. The teacher should not stand in glaring light or with his or her back to an open window, as this interferes with effective lip reading.

4. If the student appears to be inattentive or not following your instruction, make certain that the student's hearing aid is turned on.

5. The teacher should use complete but brief sentences during instruction.

6. Reduce the background noise as much as possible.

7. Articulate clearly, but do not talk louder unless you have an unusually soft voice.

8. Make certain to have the student's attention before taking or starting a lesson.

9. Speak normally. Do not over-enunciate words, speak louder than usual, or use forced facial expressions.

10. Do not chew gum or cover you mouth when talking.

11. Use visual aids whenever possible; an overhead projector is preferable to a blackboard.

12. The teacher should familiarize the student with new vocabulary prior to introducing the new topic in class.

13. Repeat and restate information by paraphrasing.

Tips for Teachers of Students With Speech and/or Language Impairments

1. Be alert to the presence of speech or language disorders.

2. Refer children suspected of having a communicative disorder to an SLP (speech-language pathologist).

3. Remember that children with speech or language disorders have difficulty communication with others.

4. Work with the SLP to integrate appropriate language development activities in all academic instruction.

5. Incorporate activities in class that allow children to practice skills mastered in therapy.

6. Always consider the developmental stage of the child suspected of having a communicative disorder before making a referral.

7. Create a supportive environment where children are encouraged to communicate with each other.

8. Create a section of the classroom where the physical environment—perhaps a large, round table—encourages sharing and discussion.

9. Provide opportunities where children feel free to exchange ideas and discuss what they are learning in different subjects.

10. Arrange for activities where children use oral language for different purposes (making a speech, leading a discussion) with different audiences (classmates, children in different classes).

11. Build self-confidence in all children, particularly those with communicative disorders. (Smith & Luckasson, 1992, p. 191)

FORM 3.1   Selecting the Least Restrictive Environment Checklist

Directions: Read each statement below and check only the statement or statements that apply the student at the present time. Complete the summary at the bottom of the page based on the responses.

Student Name: _____   Date: _____

Team Signatures:

_____   _____

_____   _____

_____   _____

_____The student's educational needs can be met in the general education classroom with mild modifications to the instructional program.

_____The general education environment will impede the student's learning.

_____The student possesses the foundation or prerequisite academic skills necessary to be successful in the general classroom.

_____The student possesses the social skills necessary to foster healthy peer relationships.

_____The student demonstrates frequent on-task behavior.

_____The student demonstrates adequate study skills.

_____The student can follow classroom rules and understands the consequence of misbehavior.

_____The student possesses a desire to be with students who do not have disabilities.

_____The student's behavior in the regular education classroom will not impair the education of students who do not have disabilities.

Summary:

_____The student would benefit from receiving his or her primary academic instruction in the regular education classroom for the areas circled below:

Circle Recommendations: Reading   English   Math   Science   Social Studies
         Other:_____

_____The student would benefit from participating in nonacademic activities in the regular education classroom for the activities circled below:

Circle Recommendations: Recess   Lunch   Assemblies   Clubs   Music   Art   Computer
         Other:_____

_____The student would not benefit from an inclusive setting at this time.

FORM 3.2   Teacher Summary Report

Directions: Please describe in detail how the student interacts and performs in your classroom on an average basis. The information will be utilized by the IEP team in order to facilitate the decision-making process in terms of appropriate inclusive settings for the student.

Student Name:_____   Date:_____

Teacher:_____

Class:_____   Period:_____

_____

_____

_____

_____

_____

_____

_____

_____

_____

_____

_____

_____

_____

_____

_____

_____

_____

_____

_____

_____

Please return to:_____

Due date:_____

FORM 3.3   Classroom Adaptations

Student Name:_____   Date:_____

Grade:_____   Subject:_____   Period:_____

Regular Education Teacher: _____

Special Education Teacher: _____

Note: The classroom adaptations checked below should be implemented in order for the student to experience success in his or her regular education class or classes. The modifications selected are in compliance with the student's IEP. In addition, the modifications are appropriate based on the student's identified and documented learning needs.

_____Preferential seating

_____Modified tests (Circle):
  – Oral Tests
  – Open book tests
  – Shortened tests
  – Eliminate choices on multiple choice tests
  – Extended time to complete tests
  – Tests may be read to student

_____Written assignments may be taped.

_____Student may leave class for assistance from his or her special education teacher (This Must Be Arranged in Advance!)

_____Give directions verbally and in written form.

_____Modified assignments (Circle):
  – Shortened assignments (fewer math problems, fewer pages to read, etc.).
  – Extended time for assignment completion.
  – Allow student to utilize several alternatives to obtain information for reports: tapes, interviews, reading, experience, etc.

_____Praise or reward student for appropriate behavior.

_____Assignment book.

_____Mark student's correct and acceptable work only.

_____ Note-taking assistance.

_____ Recognize and give credit for student's oral participation in class.

_____ Utilize cross-age tutoring.

_____ Avoid placing student under pressure of time or competition.

_____ Student may utilize cursive or manuscript writing.

_____ Utilize a behavior point system.

_____ Quietly repeat directions to student.

_____ Taped text or lectures.

_____ Special equipment needed or recommended modifications: (List)

_____

FORM 3.4   Classroom Adaptations Evaluation

Student Name:_____   Date:_____

Regular Education Class:_____   Period:_____

Regular Education Teacher:_____

Directions: List the adaptations that were implemented in the general education environment in order to meet the needs of the inclusive student. Record and discuss the results of each and use the Comments section to note all pertinent information.

Start Date	End Date	Adaptations	Results	Comments

FORM 3.5   Student's Materials List

Student Name:_____   Date:_____

The items checked below are recommended for your regular education class or classes:

_____Three-ring binder with subject dividers   Additional materials:

_____Trapper Keeper   _____

_____Pencils   _____

_____Ink pens   _____

_____Assignment book   _____

_____Paper   _____

_____Pocket folders   _____

_____Book bag   _____

_____Calculator   _____

_____Math compass   _____

_____Graph paper   _____

_____Glue   _____

_____Scissors   _____

_____Crayons   _____

_____Colored markers   _____

_____Colored pencils   _____

_____Index cards   _____

_____Spiral notebook   _____

Parent signature:_____   Date: _____

FORM 3.6A   Teacher Directions for Completing Student Monitor Form

The special education teacher should periodically monitor all students placed in inclusion or mainstreamed settings in order to address problems before they escalate and affect student performance. One of the most time-efficient methods of monitoring students is by way of a checklist. The authors have developed a monitor checklist for general education teachers. This checklist can be quickly completed by the teachers and provides a total view of student performance in the general education classroom. Please review the following directions before distributing the Student Monitor Information to teachers who instruct students with disabilities.

Directions:

1. Complete the top portion of the monitor form and distribute to each teacher of the inclusive student.

2. Monitor forms should be given to each teacher at the minimum of every three weeks or between each official school reporting period.

3. Explain to each teacher that the information completed on the form will be shared with the student and the parent when appropriate.

4. Upon receiving a monitor form that indicates areas of concerns, consult with teacher as soon as possible.

5. Arrange conference as soon as possible when concerns are of significant magnitude.

6. Special education teachers should maintain a folder of all monitor forms for documentation purposes.

7. Monitor forms should be reviewed at the annual individualized education program team meeting.

FORM 3.6B   Student Monitor Information

Student: _____   Date: _____

Subject: _____   Teacher: _____

NOTE: The information recorded on this monitor form will be shared with the student and his or her parents/guardians when appropriate and filed for documentation.

Class participation	Pass: _____	Fail: _____
Class or daily work:	Pass: _____	Fail: _____
Homework:	Pass: _____	Fail: _____
Quiz grades:	Pass: _____	Fail: _____
Test grades:	Pass: _____	Fail: _____
On-task behavior:	Good: _____	Fair: _____ Poor: _____
Tardy/absent:	T: _____	AB: _____
Overall performance:	Pass: _____	Fail: _____
Teacher request conference:	Yes: _____	No: _____

Teacher concerns:

_____

_____

_____

_____

_____

_____

_____

_____

_____

Return form to: _____

Due date: _____

FORM 3.7 Student Monitor Results Summary

Student Name: _____   Report Date: _____

Report Period: _____

NOTE: This form is to be used as a summary for the Student Monitor Information Form (Form 3.6b). Review each student's completed monitor form and place check marks in the problem areas for each subject. The summary form is a quick reference to a student's progress in an inclusion or mainstreamed setting.

Subject	Class Participation	Daily Class work	Daily Home work	Quiz Grades	Test Grades	On-Task Behavior	Overall Performance	Tardy	Absent

FORM 3.8   Individual Student Progress Report Summary

Student Name: _____

Report Period: _____

Directions: The special education teacher should record all grades that his or her students receive in their inclusion or mainstreamed classes during the progress report time period. Schools usually issue a formal progress report halfway through each reporting period. The authors strongly recommend that the teacher highlight all subjects in which students receives a grade of "D" or "F."

Student Name	Language Arts	Mathematics	Science	Social Studies	Physical Education	Elective or Exploratory

FORM 3.9   Individual Student Final Grade Summary

Student Name:_____

Semester_____   School Year:_____

Academic Subject	First Reporting Period Average	Second Reporting Period Average	Third Reporting Period Average	Semester Exam Grade	Days Absent	Conduct Average	Teacher's Comment

Additional Information:

_____

_____

_____

_____

_____

_____

_____

_____

_____

_____

_____

_____

_____

RESOURCE 3.1   Defining Accommodations and Modifications

Accommodations

Adams (1997; as cited in Polloway, Epstein, & Bursuck, 2003) defined *accommodations* as the changes in input and output processes in teaching and assessment, such as the format of instructional presentations and test practice and/or preparation activities, the setting for a test, the scheduling or timing of instruction or assessment, and the response format called for in an assessment procedure.

Modifications

According to Polloway and colleagues (2003), "The concept of modifications refers to changes in content and/or standards. In curricular areas, modifications could involve changes in content and/or skill expectations for different groups of students. A key testing modification would be limiting the amount of material upon which a student is evaluated" (p. 190).

Managing
the Classroom

In an effective classroom students should not only know what they are doing, they should also know why and how.

—Harry Wong

The teacher must create and maintain an environment in the classroom that is conducive to learning. An effective classroom management plan is the key to a strong instructional program and plays a critical role in the learning process for all students. A tremendous amount of diversity exists among special education programs and delivery models; the beginning teacher, however, must have a working knowledge of the basic components of an effective classroom management plan regardless of his or her current position. The teacher should be able to apply this knowledge to a variety of educational settings, including the general education classroom. Classroom management is defined as "a complex task consisting of planning lessons, providing safe environments, teaching students, and perhaps the most daunting task of all, appropriately responding to student behavior problems" (Backes & Ellis, 2003, p. 23). Marzano and Marzano (2003) state that, "Research has shown us that teachers' actions in their classrooms have twice the impact on student achievement as do school policies regarding curriculum, assessment, staff collegiality, and community involvement. We also know that one of the classroom teacher's most important jobs is managing the classroom" (p. 6). The components of a comprehensive classroom management plan that promotes student learning are as follows:

- The physical arrangement and decor of the classroom are inviting and conducive to learning.
- The classroom climate is supportive and reflects a sense of mutual respect between teacher and students.

- The teacher communicates the expectations for students' academic performances and behaviors in the classroom.
- The classroom's policies and procedures clearly regulate all activities.

The task of developing a classroom management plan must be accomplished prior to the start of the school year and in place on the first day of school in order to promote a positive learning environment and prevent total chaos. The plan should reflect the basic educational philosophy of the teacher, be appropriate for the student population, and be approved by the school's principal. The authors recommend that the beginning teacher enlist the assistance of a veteran teacher, possibly a mentor, when developing his or her first classroom management system. Veteran teachers are great sources of information and usually have insight into "what works" based on their own experiences.

In the following sections, the authors present a six-step process that is designed to assist the first-year teacher in developing a comprehensive and effective classroom management plan. The authors identify and present the critical components of an effective plan and provide the beginning teacher with strategies designed to support each component. The process includes requiring the teacher to review his or her school's policies pertaining teachers and students before developing and implementing his or her first plan and evaluating the success of the plan at the end of the school year. The authors provide the reader with supplemental checklists, forms, and information that will assist and support the new special education teacher in this endeavor.

STEP 1: REVIEW THE SCHOOL'S POLICIES AND PROCEDURES PERTAINING TO STUDENT AND TEACHER EXPECTATIONS

The teacher's management plan must fit within the framework of his or her assigned school's policies. Most schools have faculty and student handbooks that contain a wealth of information and prove to be a quick reference for school expectations. The teacher should obtain a copy of the student handbook and read all policies that relate to academic requirements, dress code, rules and consequences, and other miscellaneous information that should be incorporated into his or her plan. The authors recommend that the beginning teacher read and possibly memorize the faculty handbook once hired for his or her current position. The faculty handbook is the compass that enables the new teacher to chart a course toward an appropriate classroom management plan.

STEP 2: ENSURE THE PHYSICAL ARRANGEMENT AND DÉCOR OF THE CLASSROOM ARE INVITING AND CONDUCIVE TO LEARNING

The teacher must consider several environmental factors when designing his or her classroom. The classroom's physical arrangement, color scheme, bulletin board designs, temperature, lighting, and space are all factors found to impact student learning. Students' desks or tables should be arranged in a manner that allows the teacher to move among students with ease and promotes student-centered instruction. The classroom's walls should be light in hue in order to provide a pleasant backdrop for instruction. Bulletin boards can typically be found inside and/or outside the classroom and are excellent tools for reinforcing academic skills, showcasing students' best works, and reinforcing positive student behaviors. The teacher should select and utilize contrasting colors when decorating class bulletin boards. Colors that contrast with one another on the color wheel are stimulating in nature (e.g., blue and orange) while colors that are next to one another on the color wheel are calming in nature (e.g., peach and rose). The authors suggest that teachers enlist the help of their students in designing and constructing the bulletin boards in the classroom. The room temperature and lighting are two factors that also impact student learning. The room temperature and lighting must be at a level that does not impede student performance. In terms of space, earlier studies (e.g., Berdine & Cegelka, 1980; Mercer & Mercer, 1998 as cited in Lewis & Doorlag, 2003) have found that classroom space should be divided into performance areas or zones to accommodate routine activities and tasks. The teacher should modify or adapt all classroom designs to accommodate the needs of students with disabilities.

Materials or Resources:

Resource 4.1 Tips for Classroom Arrangement

Resource 4.2 Bulletin Board Guidelines and Information

STEP 3: ENSURE THE CLASSROOM CLIMATE IS SUPPORTIVE AND REFLECTS A SENSE OF MUTUAL RESPECT BETWEEN TEACHER AND STUDENTS

The classroom climate must be supportive and reflect a sense of mutual respect among all stakeholders in order to foster the learning process. Marzano and Marzano (2003) conducted studies on the quality of teacher–student relationships and found that "teachers who had high-quality relationships with their students had 31 percent fewer discipline problems, rule violations, and related problems over a year's time than did teachers who did not have the same relationship"(p. 6). The purpose of establishing quality relationships with students is not only to prevent or decrease discipline issues, but to convey to students that the classroom is a safe place to try newly acquired skills. In addition, Backes and Ellis (2003) state, "A key element in assuming leadership of a classroom is to convey to students that they are important and that the teacher is confident that they can master the content" (p. 23). There will be occasions when conflict in the classroom will arise and threaten to diminish the supportive climate and damage relationships among members of the classroom. Teachers must address and resolve conflicts in a timely manner. The teacher can utilize individual student conferences when the conflict involves only a few students; however, the authors have found holding a class meeting is extremely effective when the conflict involves a large group of students. Class meetings allow students to discuss problem areas without ridicule and develop solutions to resolve conflicts. The teacher is the facilitator and lays the ground rules for all meetings at the beginning of the school year. The teacher may also have to address bullying and harassment of students at some time during the school year. These are major issues that can lead to serious consequences if not addressed expeditiously by the teacher. Many school systems have specific policies and procedures regarding these areas, and the teacher must familiarize himself or herself with this information. According to McNamara (as cited in Salend, 2001), "You may need to deal with bullying or peer harassment, which may take the form of extorting lunch money, taunting, name-calling, spreading false rumors, and using verbal and physical threats" (p. 258). The authors suggest that the beginning teacher utilize a variety of methods and resources to convey to students that they are valuable members of the classroom.

STEP 4: COMMUNICATE ALL EXPECTATIONS FOR STUDENTS' ACADEMIC PERFORMANCES AND BEHAVIORS IN THE CLASSROOM

The authors advise the new teacher to thoroughly explain and discuss classroom expectations with students as soon as possible. "Communication, both nonverbal and verbal, is the 'stuff' that initiates, builds, maintains, and destroys relationships" (Miller, Wackman, Nunnally, & Miller, 1988, p. 9). Teachers must "raise the bar" in terms of setting high expectations for the academic performance of all students. The teacher must clearly define acceptable and unacceptable student work and challenge students to meet his or her expectations. Teachers must both celebrate students' successes, and provide encouragement when a student's mastery of learning objectives is not achieved.

In terms of student behavior, the new teacher must also set high expectations for all students and clearly define both acceptable and unacceptable behavior during the first days of the new school year. The establishment of well-defined behavior expectations is essential to maintaining a sense of order in the classroom. The new teacher must select an approach to classroom discipline that does not conflict with his or her school's schoolwide discipline plan and own personal educational philosophy, and that fits the identified needs of the educational program.

There are numerous discipline approaches available for the new teacher to review. The authors suggest that the first-year teacher review the following programs:

- Love and Logic (2008): www.loveandlogic.com
- Discipline With Dignity (n.d.): www.tlc-sems.com/Discipline-With-Dignity.aspx
- Assertive Discipline (Canter, n.d.): http://campus.dyc.edu/~drwaltz/FoundLearnTheory/FLT_readings/Canter.htm
- Behavior Analysis (Watson, 2008): http://specialed.about.com/od/specialedacronyms/g/aba.htm
- Linda Albert's Cooperative Discipline (*The Three C's*, n.d.): http://members.tripod.com/tkmoyer/CooperativeDiscipline/id17.htm

The authors recommend that the first-year special education teacher develop a classroom discipline plan prior to the start of the school year. Suggestions for developing rules and consequences and behavior management plans are included at the end of the chapter. The new teacher should obtain approval from the school principal for all classroom discipline plans and behavior modification strategies prior to implementation.

Materials or Resources:

Resource 4.3 Tips for Communicating With Students and Parents

Form 4.1 Daily Point System

Form 4.2 Behavior Contract

Form 4.3 Student Progress Report

STEP 5: DEVELOP CLASSROOM POLICIES AND PROCEDURES THAT CLEARLY REGULATE ALL ACTIVITIES

According to Harry Wong (1991), "Effective teachers spend a good deal of time the first weeks of the school year introducing, teaching, modeling, and practicing procedures until they become routines" (p. 1). The establishing of policies and procedures is extremely important to the basic operation of the special education classroom. The new teacher must understand the difference between the two terms before developing his or her plan of action. Classroom *procedures* are designated methods for completing certain class activities or tasks. The teacher can think of classroom procedures as the way to "conduct business" in the classroom. Classroom *policies* are a set of guiding principles or courses of action. The authors recommend that the teacher review the Classroom Policies and Procedures Checklist located at the end of the chapter and select the activities or issues that apply to his or her current teaching situation. The authors suggest that the teacher add items as needed at the end of the list.

Materials or Resources:

Form 4.4 Classroom Policies and Procedures Checklist

STEP 6: EVALUATE THE OVERALL EFFECTIVENESS OF THE CLASSROOM MANAGEMENT PLAN

The authors strongly encourage the beginning teacher to evaluate his or her classroom management plan at the end of the school year. The evaluation process can be a matter of self-reflection or may also include an informal survey of students and parents. The authors have found that the evaluation is more meaningful when all stakeholders have been included in the process. The authors provide a sample evaluation form at the end of the chapter. The form is basic in design and may be revised to best meet the needs of the teacher and older students.

Materials or Resources:

Form 4.5 Classroom Management Plan Evaluation

FORM 4.1   Daily Point System

Week of:_____

Class:_____   Period:_____

Directions: List the names of the students in your class. Place check marks when a student exhibits a listed behavior. The results can be utilized as part of a reward system established by the classroom teacher.

Classroom Behaviors						
Student Name	On Time to Class	Prepared for Class: Pencil Paper Homework Textbook Notebook	Works Quietly In Class	Stays on Task	Participates in Class	TOTAL *POINTS*

FORM 4.2   Behavior Contract

Student Name: _____   Date: _____

Teacher Name: _____   Class: _____

Contract Starts: _____   Contract Ends: _____

Contract Review Dates: _____   _____   _____   _____   _____   _____

The student will

_____

_____

_____

_____

_____

_____

Teacher will

_____

_____

_____

_____

_____

The student must fulfill his or her part of the contract in order to receive the agreed-upon reward from the teacher.

Student Signature: _____

Teacher Signature: _____

Parent/Guardian Signature: _____

FORM 4.3 Student Progress Report

Student Name:_____   Date:_____

> Directions: Please check the column that accurately depicts the student's progress in the subject and behavior columns and provide comments where necessary.

Subject/Behavior	Satisfactory	Needs Improvement
Reading		
English		
Math		
Science		
Social Studies		
Written Expression		
Follows class rules		
Exhibits appropriate behavior both inside and outside of class		
Respects personal and school property		
Participates in class		
Completes assigned work		
Follows directions		
Brings materials to class		

Student Signature:_____

Teacher Signature:_____

Parent Signature:_____

FORM 4.4   Classroom Policies and Procedures Checklist

Classroom Procedures Are Needed For:

_____ How students are to enter the classroom

_____ How students are to exit the classroom

_____ How and when students will be excused to the restroom

_____ How and when students will get a drink of water

_____ Class schedule for academics or specialty classes

_____ How students are to respond or ask questions in the classroom

_____ How and when students will move around in the classroom

_____ Specify appropriate student behavior when working with other students

_____ Where students are to place personal items: Book bags, coats, lunch boxes, and more.

_____ How teacher will collect monies: Lunch, fieldtrip, book fines, and so on.

_____ How students are to move in the hallway

_____ Other:_____

Classroom Policies Are Needed For:

_____ Grading system or method

_____ Late work

_____ Class work

_____ Makeup work

_____ Homework

_____ Student tardiness

_____ Student attendance

_____ Reporting student progress

_____ Reporting student final grade

_____ Required class materials

_____ Assessment of students in the special and inclusive classroom

_____ Other:_____

FORM 4.5   Classroom Management Plan Evaluation

School Year: _____

Directions: I would appreciate your assistance with an important project that will help me make our classroom a better place to learn. PLEASE MAKE A LIST OF WHAT YOU LIKE BEST AND WHAT YOU WOULD LIKE TO CHANGE ABOUT OUR CLASSROOM. I have listed some areas you might want to consider at the bottom of the page. Thank you!

The things I like best about our classroom.	The things I would like to change in our classroom.

Areas to consider:

- Classroom color
- Classroom arrangement
- Seating arrangement
- Classroom rules and consequences
- Classroom policies and procedures (for example, how the teacher grades, how quickly the teacher returns completed work, etc.)
- Class activities
- Class games and materials
- Class field trips
- How the teacher communicates with me

RESOURCE 4.1   Tips for Classroom Arrangement

- Ensure the classroom is barrier free and safe for students.

- Designate specific areas of the classroom for specific activities:

    Main instruction area

    Small group instruction area

    Learning centers area

    Computer or technology area

    Free reading area

    Reference book area

    Teacher instructional materials area

    Student materials area

    Independent study area

    Listening center area

    Teacher storage area

- Place teacher's desk in the best location to monitor students and least likely to interfere with instruction.

- Place paraprofessional's desk area in the best area to assist students.

- Arrange students' desks in a manner that is conducive to student-centered instruction.

RESOURCE 4.2   Bulletin Board Guidelines and Information

- Bulletin boards can be used for a variety of purposes:
  - Displaying student work (neatly)
  - Displaying class schedule
  - Displaying monthly calendar
  - Posting of school news
  - Extension of instructional unit or theme
  - Aiding in instruction/reinforce skill
  - Posting notices
  - Decorating the classroom
  - Displaying word of the day
- Commercial or teacher-made materials can be used
- Materials should be laminated for durability
- Make titles for bulletin boards to explain themes or purposes
- Use contrasting colors
- Bulletin boards are appropriate for all age groups
- Designate a storage place for all bulletin board materials

RESOURCE 4.3 Tips for Communicating With Students and Parents

- Certificates and awards
- Class meetings
- Daily progress report
- Display students' best work on a special bulletin board
- Individual conference with student
- Positive notes to parents or guardians
- Positive notes to students
- Positive sticker on a good paper
- Positive telephone calls or e-mails to parents or guardians
- Recognize acts of kindness toward other classmates
- Special class privileges
- Tangible rewards
- Teacher–student conferences
- Verbal praise
- Weekly progress report

Teaching All Students

When we work from the conviction that all children can learn, when we set high expectations, and we strengthen the curriculum, students rise to meet the challenges.

—Richard Riley

Teachers across the United States are confronting a multitude of challenges in their journeys to prepare students to meet the demands of rigorous standards-based curriculums and to compete in a global economy. While teachers continue to struggle with issues revolving around high dropout rates, chronic absenteeism, and serious discipline problems of students, the No Child Left Behind Act (NCLB) is the challenge that is currently at the forefront for most educators. NCLB has placed an enormous amount of pressure on teachers to increase the academic achievement of all students, including students with disabilities. Special education teachers have been significantly touched by NCLB and thrust into the accountability arena with their general education colleagues. The movement across the nation of placing and educating more students with disabilities in general education classrooms or least restrictive environments is causing special education teachers to make necessary paradigm shifts. No longer can the special education teacher think in terms of "What instructional practices and strategies can I use to effectively meet the needs of my students with disabilities?" but instead he or she must think in terms of "What instructional practices and strategies can I use to meet the needs of all students?" Both general and special education teachers must become data savvy and routinely begin to use qualitative and quantitative data for the purpose of instructional decision making and evaluating student progress. Teachers must arm themselves with the knowledge of how to interpret and use data in order to meet the accountability challenge.

The information contained in this chapter is designed to guide the beginning teacher through the planning and implementation of instruction for all students. The authors acknowledge that diversity exists among special education programs and delivery models; however, the authors contend that the information provided in this chapter can be applied to most educational settings or programs to include the general education classroom. The authors provide the reader with the basic steps of instructional planning and implementation that will provide the framework for a successful teaching experience and list effective instructional strategies designed to reach all students. In addition, the final section of the chapter pertains to standards-based classrooms, and the information will give the reader a general overview of the concept. The authors have included all forms and resource information at the end of the chapter that will support the new teacher.

SECTION 1: PREPARING FOR INSTRUCTION

Step 1: Review the Individualized Education Program

The individualized education program (IEP) is the foundation and driving force behind all academic instruction for students with disabilities. The teacher must review each student's IEP and identify the academic goals and objectives that must be addressed prior to the first day of school. The authors have developed an IEP Goals and Objectives Checklist (see Form 5.1) designed to assist the beginning teacher with instructional planning. After completing the checklist, the teacher should be able to map out his or her direction for academic instruction, select appropriate instructional materials, and create lesson plans that incorporate the instructional strategies and evaluation methods prescribed in each student's plan. The new teacher must review each student's IEP and complete the following tasks before planning and implementing his or her instructional plans:

- Identify specific academic skills and course standards to be taught
- Identify specific methods and materials to be used in the instructional process
- Identify specific methods and materials to be used to monitor progress and evaluate each goal and objective
- Review the initiation and completion dates of all goals and objectives
- Identify the specific provider/providers for all academic areas in which the student is served

Step 2: Select Instructional Materials

The special education teacher must begin the process of selecting instructional materials after reviewing each student's current IEP. The selection process can seem somewhat overwhelming and confusing for the new special education teacher; however, Mercer and Mercer (1993) suggest that teachers utilize the following plan when selecting instructional materials:

- Identify the curriculum areas in which materials are needed.
- Rank the areas form highest to lowest priority.
- List affordable materials that are designed to teach in the selected skill area or areas.
- Obtain the materials and evaluate them so that a decision can be made regarding a purchase. On request, many publishers will provide a sample of materials or a manual for the teacher to examine or field test. Also, many school districts have resource or curriculum centers that contain materials for teachers to inspect. (p. 150)

The teacher should review and select instructional materials that are appropriate for students with disabilities and support the curriculum for the designated subject or skill areas. The authors strongly recommend that the new teacher use the instructional materials available in his or her school system when appropriate. These materials have usually been thoroughly reviewed and found to support the system's and state approved curriculum. In most instances, students who are served in general education classrooms and are expected to take the same standardized assessments as their nondisabled peers should be expected to use the same course materials. In addition, the authors recommend that the new teacher consult with other teachers on staff for advice and guidance in the selection and location of instructional materials. The authors have created the Classroom Teacher's Instructional Materials List (see Form 5.2) to use during the selection process, and they provide the reader with a list of commercial publishers (see Resource 5.1).

Step 3: Creating a Class Schedule

The new teacher must create a class schedule that is appropriate for his or her program or delivery model. Class schedules vary greatly among the various special education models and programs and between different grade levels. The special education teacher should design a class schedule that flows with the school's master schedule, is conducive to the schedules of inclusive students, and allows for teacher planning. Teachers in resource or self-contained settings should design a schedule that will accommodate academic instruction; students in inclusive classes; specialty, exploratory, or elective classes; lunch; and recess (when appropriate). An effective schedule is vital to the overall operation of the special education classroom. The class schedule provides structure, ensures that instruction time for the core academic areas is maximized, and integrates lower priority classes with other miscellaneous activities. The authors list some suggestions for class schedules based on grade level.

Elementary Level

- Analyze the day's events
- Plan opening exercises
- Schedule academic instruction
- Plan closing exercises (Mercer & Mercer, 1993, p. 128)

Secondary Level

- Homeroom
- Academic instruction: school day is divided into class periods (possibly 6–7 classes a day/50–55 minutes per class)
- Lunch
- Exploratory class (middle school)
- Elective class (high school)
- Transition program
- Planning
- Advisement

Materials or Resources:

Form 5.1 IEP Goals and Objectives Checklist

Form 5.2 Classroom Teacher's Instructional Materials List

Form 5.3 Class Schedule

Resource 5.1 Guide to Locating Instructional Materials

SECTION 2: PLANNING AND IMPLEMENTING EFFECTIVE LESSON PLANS

The teacher should plan and implement lesson plans that take into consideration how each student receives and processes information, and how the lesson plans address the need of the student, promote a sense of wonder and excitement within the student, and engage the student in the learning process. This section provides some hints for better lesson planning and implementation; however, the authors suggest that the teacher use the information listed below as a basic framework and then eventually develop a system that fits his or her personal style. The authors have included a Weekly Lesson Plan (see Form 5.4) that the teacher may use when planning for instruction.

Instructional Planning Guide

- Plan lessons at least two weeks in advance.
- Set aside time each day to plan—don't try to do all your planning in one day.
- Collaborate and plan with the primary teacher in inclusive settings.
- Review the objectives or standards for each lesson to be taught.
- Develop essential questions and enduring understandings for each lesson or unit.
- Post essential questions and enduring understandings in highly visible location.
- Select supporting materials to reinforce lesson objectives or standards being taught.
- Make copies of all reinforcement materials in advance.

- Write all plans in a lesson plan book or in the format required by your school.
- Give a copy of your lesson plans to the designated person at your school as required.
- Secure all additional materials for the lesson in advance (e.g., videos, maps, and calculators).
- Prepare a weekly syllabus or homework calendar for students.
- Inform students in advance of all test dates.
- Make sure overhead or LCD projector and other pieces of equipment are in working order in advance of lesson presentation.
- Review all lessons prior to implementation.

Implementation of Lesson Plans:

Preview Lesson

- Introduce lesson or skill using essential questions and enduring understandings
- Administer a diagnostic assessment or require students to complete a KWL chart (what I know, what I want to know, what I learned) if beginning a new unit
- Review previous lesson (make a link to prior knowledge)
- Preteach lesson vocabulary

Lesson Content

- Demonstrate skill and/or standard; explain and discuss with students
- Provide opportunity for guided practice; correct and discuss
- Provide opportunity for independent practice; correct and discuss
- Provide opportunity for students to demonstrate skill (i.e., presentation, product)
- Administer formative assessment, check on learning
- Reteach problem areas and determine next steps

Lesson Conclusion

- Summarize lesson/review enduring understandings
- Answer essential questions
- Administer summative assessment, determine skills or standards mastery

Materials and Resources

Form 5.4 Weekly Lesson Plan

Resource 5.2 Technology-Connected Lesson Plan

SECTION 3: INSTRUCTIONAL STRATEGIES FOR ALL STUDENTS

In this section, the authors provide the new teacher with instructional strategies that can be utilized with special and general education students. The strategies can be modified to fit the individual needs of students when appropriate. The authors provide a reference for each set of instructional strategies.

Strategy 1: Differentiated Instruction

Differentiation is a teaching concept in which the classroom teacher plans for the diverse needs of students. The teacher must consider such differences as the students':

1. Learning styles, skill levels, and rates
2. Learning difficulties
3. Language proficiency
4. Background experiences and knowledge
5. Interests
6. Motivation
7. Ability to attend
8. Social and emotional development
9. Various intelligences
10. Levels of abstraction
11. Physical needs (Walker, 2007, slide 7)

Four Ways to Differentiate Instruction:

1. Differentiating the content/topic
2. Differentiating the process/activities
3. Differentiating the product
4. Differentiating by manipulating the environment or through accommodating individual learning styles (Walker, 2007, slide 17)

Strategy 2: Teacher-Directed Instruction

"In a teacher-directed classroom, the teacher plans, shapes and guides the learning process. He or she analyzes course standards and prepares a sequence of instructional strategies to help students acquire the knowledge and skills to met those standards" (Tanner, Bottoms, & Bearman, 2001, p. 6).

Strategy 3: Student-Centered Learning

"Student-centered learning is based on the belief that active involvement by students increases learning and motivation. Good student-centered learning values the student's role in acquiring knowledge and understanding" (Tanner, Bottoms, & Bearman, 2001, p. 8).

Strategy 4: Graphic Organizers

Graphic organizers are instructional tools that facilitate instruction and promote student learning (Figure 5.1). Graphic organizers can be defined as the following:

1. Graphic organizers help students comprehend information through visual representations of concepts, ideas, and relationships. They provide the structure for short- and long-term memory.

2. Graphic organizers turn abstract concepts into concrete visual representations.

3. Understanding text structure is critical to reading comprehension. If students have a guide to the text structure, their comprehension is considerably higher than when they rely only on reading and memorization.

4. The most important question a teacher can answer is: "How do I want students to think about my content?" Then, the teacher selects a graphic organizer that facilitates that type of thinking. (Thompson & Thompson, 2003, p. 2)

Figure 5.1   Graphic Organizer Sample: Compare and Contrast

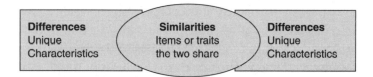

Strategy 5: Strategies for Summarizing Learning:

According to Max and Julia Thompson (2003), having students summarize is important to the learning process for the following reasons:

1. Summarizing is perhaps the key thinking skill for learning.

2. Summarizing is a learning strategy, not a teaching strategy. Learners must summarize themselves for the learning to construct meaning.

3. When summarizing, students create a "schema" for the information and remember it better and longer.

4. Teachers find out what students have internalized, understood, and remembered.

5. When students summarize, their confusions, misconceptions, or misunderstandings surface, and teachers can then adapt future teaching accordingly. It is key to knowing when and on what to reteach.

6. Student summarizing should be distributed through a lesson, not just at the end. (Thompson & Thompson, 2003, p. 2)

SECTION 4: EVALUATING STUDENT PROGRESS

The evaluation of student progress and mastery of academic skills and standards is an essential step in the instructional process. The beginning teacher will quickly discover that the best way to obtain a total picture of a student's level of mastery is to utilize a variety of assessments. Assessments can be classified as formative and summative. Formative assessments are usually given to students in order to determine their levels of understanding of the concepts being taught, and the results provide the teacher with insight into any instructional adjustments that need to be made. Levy (2008) states that "summative assessment is used to determine whether the student has successfully learned what was taught" (p. 163). The authors have found that performance-based assessments, which are formative in nature, are extremely useful in assessing student learning. Performance-based assessments require students to demonstrate their knowledge of acquired skills. According to the Spring 1996 issue of the newsletter, *Improving America's School: A Newsletter on Issues in School Reform* (U.S. Department of Education, 1996), performance assessments may include any of the following categories of items:

> **Open-ended or constructed response items** that ask students to respond in their own words—to "construct" their answers—to questions that may have multiple good answers. Students usually reason out their solutions as part of their answers. Usually students can answer these questions in just a few minutes, and in that way they differ from some of the performance activities described below.
>
> **Performance-based items or events:** questions, tasks, or activities that require students to perform an action. Although performances can involve demonstrations or presentations, most typically they involve students explaining how they would answer the question or solve a problem by writing a few sentences or paragraphs, drawing and explaining a diagram, or performing an experiment. Such tasks may take from 15 minutes to an hour or more and may involve some work with a group of students who think through the answers and later provide their own individually written answers.
>
> **Projects or experiments:** extended performance tasks that may take several days or even several weeks to complete. Students generate problems, consider options, propose solutions, and demonstrate their solutions. Students often work in groups, at least for some of the project, to analyze options and to consider ways to present their thinking and conclusions.
>
> **Portfolios:** collections of student work that show teachers and others who may "score" portfolios the range and quality of student work over a period of time and in various content areas. There are almost as many approaches to compiling and evaluating portfolios as there are proponents of this form of assessment. Portfolios can be used both formally and informally; ideally, portfolios capture the evolution of students' ideas and can be used instructionally and as progress markers for students, teachers, and program evaluators. (U.S. Department of Education, 1996, pp. 1, 2)

SECTION 5: DEFINING
A STANDARDS-BASED CLASSROOM

States are aggressively developing and implementing rigorous curriculum standards in core subject areas in an effort to better prepare students to meet the demands of NCLB. Teachers make the necessary paradigm shifts in order to assist students in meeting or exceeding standards. Teachers must rethink their instructional formats and create classrooms that are standards-based ready: "A classroom where teachers and students have a clear understanding of the expectations (standards). They know what they are teaching/learning each day (standards), why the day's learning is an important thing to know or know how to do (relevance), and how to do it (process). Standards-based learning is a process, not an event" (Georgia Department of Education, n.d., slide 3).

FORM 5.1   **IEP Goals and Objectives Checklist**

Student Name:_____   School Year:_____

Directions: Complete the information below upon review of each student's current IEP.

Skill Area	Recommended Instructional Methods	Required Instructional Materials	Recommended Method of Evaluation

NOTES:_____

_____

_____

_____

_____

Skill Areas: Academic, social, daily living, leisure, transition, or other.

Instructional Method: Modeling, guided practice, reinforcements, drill and practice, use of manipulatives, chaining, whole language approach, direct instruction, learning strategies, differentiation approach, or other.

Instructional Materials: Textbooks, supporting materials, manipulatives, concrete materials, or other.

Methods of Evaluation: Observation, work samples, unit tests, surveys, interviews, criterion reference tests, student portfolios, or other.

Form 5.2   Classroom Teacher's Instructional Materials List

Teacher Name:_____   Date:_____

Program:_____   Room:_____

Skill Area	Instructional Materials (List and Describe)	Quantity Requested	Company Name, Address, Telephone Number, and Fax Number

Form 5.3 Class Schedule

Teacher:_____   SchoolYear:_____

Semester:_____

Time	Subject/Activity

Form 5.4   Weekly Lesson Plan

Class or Subject:_____   Week of:_____

Class Time:_____   Period:_____

Textbook:_____

Class Roster:

_____

_____

_____

Chapter/Topic:_____

Lesson Objectives

_____

_____

_____

Day	Activities/Content	Homework
Monday Date:		
Tuesday Date:		
Wednesday Date:		
Thursday Date:		
Friday Date:		

Notes:

_____

_____

_____

RESOURCE 5.1   Guide to Locating Instructional Materials

Academic Communication Associates, Inc.
Publication Center, Dept. 62E
4149 Avenida de la Plata
P.O. Box 4279
Oceanside, CA 92052-4279
Telephone: 760-758-9593
FAX: 760-758-1604

Academic Therapy Publications
20 Commercial Boulevard
Novato, CA 94949-6191
Telephone: 415-883-3314
FAX: 415-883-3720

Addison Wesley Longman Publishing Co.
1 Jacob Way
Reading, MA 01867
Telephone: 800-552-2499
FAX: 800-284-8292

A.D.D. Warehouse
300 NW 70th Avenue, Suite 102
Plantation, FL 33337
Telephone: 800-233-9273
FAX: 954-792-8545
Web site: www.addwarehouse.com

American Guidance Service—AGS
4201 Woodland Road
Circle Pines, MN 55014-1796
Telephone: 800-328-2560
FAX: 612-786-9077

Bureau for At-Risk Youth
135 Dupont Street
P.O. Box 760
Plainview, NY 11803-0760
Telephone: 800-999-6884
FAX: 516-349-5521
Web site: www.at-risk.com

C. H. Stoelting Co.
620 Wheat Lane
Wood Dale, IL 60191
Telephone: 630-860-9700
FAX: 630-860-9775

Cambridge Development Laboratory, Inc.
86 West Street
Waltham, MA 02451
Telephone: 800-637-0047
FAX: 781-890-2894

Capstone Curriculum Publishing
151 Good Counsel Drive
P.O. Box 669
Mankato, MN 56002-0669
Telephone: 888-574-6711
FAX: 888-574-6183

Center on Education and Work
University of Wisconsin–Madison
School of Education
964 Educational Sciences Building
1025 W. Johnson Street
Madison, WI 53706-1796
Telephone: 800-446-0399
FAX: 608-262-9197

Channing L. Bete Co., Inc.
200 State Road
South Deerfield, MA 01373-0200
Telephone: 877-896-8532
FAX: 800-499-6464
Web site: www.channing-bete.com

Child's Work Child's PLAY
Genesis Direct Inc.
100 Plaza Drive
Secaucus, NJ 07094-3613
Telephone: 800-962-1141
FAX: 201-583-3644

Curriculum Associates
5 Esquire Road, N
Billerica, MA 01862-2589
Telephone: 800-225-0248
FAX: 800-366-1158
Web site: www.curriculumassociates.com

EBSCO Curriculum Materials
Box 11521
Birmingham, AL 35202-1521
Telephone: 800-633-8623
FAX: 205-991-1482

Educational Design
345 Hudson Street
New York, NY 10014-4502
Telephone: 800-221-9372
FAX: 212-675-6922

Educators Publishing Service, Inc.
31 Smith Place
Cambridge, MA 02138
Telephone: 800-225-5750
FAX: 617-547-0412
Web site: www.epsbooks.com

Funtastic Therapy
RD 4 Box 14, John White Road
Cranberry, NJ 08512
Telephone: 800-531-3176
FAX: 609-275-0488

Glencoe/McGraw-Hill
P.O. Box 508
Columbus, OH 43216
Telephone: 800-334-7344
FAX: 614-860-1877
Web site: http://www.glencoe.com

Globe Fearon Publishers
4350 Equity Drive
P.O. Box 2649
Columbus, OH 43216
Telephone: 800-848-9500
FAX: 614-771-7361

Greenwood Publishing Group, Inc.
88 Post road West
Westport, CT 06881
Telephone: 203-226-3571
FAX: 203-222-1502
Web site: http://www.greenwood.com

Hawthorne Educational Services
800 Gray Oak Drive
Columbia, MO 65201
Telephone: 800-542-1673
FAX: 800-442-9509

Huby's Ltd.
School to Work Catalog
Department: W99
P.O. Box 9117
Jackson, WY 83002
Telephone: 800-543-0998
FAX: 800-518-2514

J. Weston Walch Publishers
321 Valley Street
P.O. Box 658
Portland, Maine 04104-0658
Telephone: 800-341-6094
Fax: 207-772-3105

Kaplan Early Learning Company
P.O. Box 609
1310 Lewisville-Clemmons Road
Lewisville, NC 27023-0609
Telephone: 800-334-2014
FAX: 800-452-7526
Web site: http://www.kaplanco.com

Lakeshore Learning Materials
2695 East Dominquez Street
P.O. Box 6261
Carson, CA 90749
Telephone: 800-421-5354
FAX: 310-537-5403
Web site: http://www.lakeshorelearning.com

PCI Education
2800 NE Loop 410, Suite 105
San Antonio, TX 78218-1525
Telephone: 800-594-4263
FAX: 888-259-8284
Web site: http://www.pcicatalog.com

Prufrock Press, Inc.
P.O. Box 8813
Waco, TX 76714-8813
Telephone: 800-998-2208
FAX: 800-240-0333
Web site: http://www.prufrock.com/

(Continued)

RESOURCE 5.1 (Continued)

Remedia Publications
15887 North 76th Street, Suite 120
Scottsdale, AZ 85260
Telephone: 800-826-4740
FAX: 602-661-9901
Web site: http://www.rempub.com

Research Press Publishers
P.O. Box 9177
Champaign, IL 61826
Telephone: 800-510-2707
FAX: 217-252-1221
Web site: http://www.researchpress.com

Resources for Educators
P.O. Box 362916
Des Moines, IA 50336-2916
Telephone: 800-491-0551
FAX: 800-835-5327

Saddleback Educational, Inc.
3503 Cadillac Avenue, Building F-9
Costa Mesa, CA 92618-2767
Telephone: 949-860-2500
FAX: 949-860-2508

Scholastic, Inc.
P.O. Box 7502
Jefferson City, MO 65102
Telephone: 800-724-6527
FAX: 573-635-7630

Scott Foresman/Addison Wesley
School Services
1 Jacob Way
Reading, MA 01867
Telephone: 800-552-2259
FAX: 800-333-3328

Slosson Educational Publications, Inc.
P.O. Box 544
East Aurora, NY 14052
Telephone: 888-756-7766
FAX: 800-655-3840
Web site: http://www.slosson.com

SRA/McGraw-Hill
220 East Danieldale Road
DeSoto, TX 75115-2490
Telephone: 800-843-8855
FAX: 214-228-1982

Teacher Ideas Press
P.O. Box 6633
Englewood, CO 80155-6633
Telephone: 800-237-6124
FAX: 303-220-8843

Things for Learning
P.O. Box 908
Rutherfordton, NC 28139
Telephone: 800-228-6178
FAX: 704-287-9506

Western Psychological Services
12031 Wilshire Boulevard
Los Angeles, CA 90025
Telephone: 800-648-8857
FAX: 310-478-7838

Wieser Educational Inc.
30085 Comercio
Rancho Santa Margarita, CA 92688-2106
Telephone: 800-880-4433
FAX: 800-949-0209

RESOURCE 5.2   Technology-Connected Lesson Plan Form

Lesson Title:_____

Subject area

Area:_____

Topic:_____

Performance Objectives

After completion of the lesson, students will be able to (use action verbs):

1._____

2._____

3._____

4._____

5._____

Lesson Format or Procedure

_____

_____

_____

_____

Assessment of Student Learning

Explain in detail how students will be assessed upon completion of lesson:

_____

_____

_____

_____

Classroom Management Strategies

_____

_____

Required Materials or Equipment

_____

_____

_____

**Related
URLs:** _____

Source: Adapted from the Georgia Department of Education—Georgia Educational Technology Training Centers *Integrating TECHnology* Lesson Plan Format.

Preparing for a Successful Parent Conference

The most basic of all human needs is the need to understand and be understood. The best way to understand people is to listen to them.

—Ralph Nichols

Typically, schools found to be high performing are ones where there is a significant level of parent involvement. A school's faculty and staff must constantly strive to build solid relationships with parents and guardians. "Communication, both nonverbal and verbal, is the 'stuff' that initiates, builds, maintains, and destroys relationships" (Miller, Wackman, Nunnally, & Miller, 1988, p. 9). A parent conference is an excellent two-way communication strategy that the new teacher can use to begin building rapport and trust with his or her students' parents or guardians. Parent conferences tend to be more personal and productive, and they provide less chance for the misinterpretation of information. In her article "Rethinking Parent Conferences," Black (2005) identifies and describes four different formats for parent conferences: traditional parent–teacher conference, arena conference, triad conference, and student-led conference (p. 47). The authors have found the traditional parent–teacher conference and student-led conference formats to be most successful. In the information that follows, the authors provide the reader with information and strategies pertaining to basic communication skills and the traditional parent–teacher and student-led conferences.

SECTION 1: HOW TO COMMUNICATE EFFECTIVELY

Typically, special education teachers conduct numerous parent conferences during the school year and organize and facilitate many more involving teachers, administrators, other support personnel, and students. The new teacher must possess the skills necessary to communicate effectively during these meetings. The teacher can perfect his or her communication skills that are essential for a successful parent conference by focusing on developing positive speaking, rephrasing, and attentive listening skills. Berger (1995) provides teachers with the following qualities of good communicators:

Give their total attention to the speaker.

1. Restate the parents' concerns.

2. Show respect for the other person.

3. Recognize the parents' feelings.

4. Tailor discussions to fit the parents' ability to handle the situation. Do not touch off the fuse of a parent who might not be able to handle a child's difficulties.

5. Emphasize that concerns are no one's fault.

6. Remember that no one ever wins an argument.

7. Protect the parents' egos.

8. Focus on one issue at a time.

9. Listen.

10. Become allies with parents. (Berger, 1995, p. 276)

Parents need to leave each conference with the feeling that someone truly understands their concerns and confidant that any plans or strategies developed during the conference will be implemented and monitored by school officials. Most often, if the new teacher uses good communication skills, rapport will be established and the foundation will be laid for a good parent–teacher relationship. Unfortunately, conferences are not always pleasant experiences for school officials or parents, and sometimes a satisfactory resolution to an identified problem or concern is elusive for all in attendance. The beginning teacher must be prepared to deal with the dissatisfaction or the anger of parents. The authors found a list of suggestions created by Michael A. Morehead to be beneficial for teachers and other school personnel when dealing with angry parents (see Resource 6.1). In addition, the authors suggest that the teacher have a school administrator attend any parent conference where he or she feels uncomfortable meeting with the parents or guardians alone or feels as though the meeting may not progress in a positive manner.

SECTION 2: UNDERSTANDING TRADITIONAL PARENT–TEACHER CONFERENCES

The objectives of a traditional parent–teacher conference depend on the purpose of the meeting. The following are conference categories most frequently used by special education teachers: progress report, problem solving, and the annual individualized education program (IEP). Minke and Anderson (2003) found two primary themes to be supported in traditional parent conferences: "Parents and teachers agreed that conferences are important opportunities for information exchange, with the major purpose of teachers giving information to parents; and parents and teachers approach conferences with varying degrees of trepidation" (p. 57). A successful parent–teacher conference requires a tremendous amount of preplanning by the teacher. The authors provide the reader with a recommended list of essential tasks that generally contribute to the success of most parent–teacher conferences and separate lists for the progress report and problem-solving conferences that will assist the teacher in his or her preparation and ensure a successful and productive parent–teacher meeting. All information pertaining to IEP conferences is located in Chapter 8. The authors provide an overview at the end of this chapter of June Million's (2005) list of the "dos and don'ts" when conducting a parent–teacher conference (see Resource 6.1).

SECTION 3: UNDERSTANDING STUDENT-LED CONFERENCES

In addition to the traditional parent–teacher conference format, the authors suggest that the beginning teacher consider the student-led format when the objective is to showcase student work or the completion of major projects. New teachers will soon discover that one of the ingredients critical to student success in the classroom is that they must take responsibility for their own learning. Students must be able to recognize quality work and know where their work stands on the continuum of meeting course standards. The student-led conference provides an opportunity for students to articulate to their parents all academic successes and failures through portfolios filled with artifacts of their learning. Hackmann (1997) reveals in his article, "Student-led Conferences at the Middle Level," the five main goals of a student-led conference:

> To encourage students to accept personal responsibility for their academic performance;
>
> to teach students the process of self-evaluation;
>
> to facilitate the development of students' organizational and oral communication skills and to increase their self-confidence;
>
> to encourage students, parents, and teachers to engage in open and honest dialogue; and
>
> to increase parent attendance at conferences. (p. 2)

The teacher serves as a facilitator during the student-led conference and intervenes only when he or she feels it is appropriate. This format may not be appropriate if the student is experiencing severe problems in the classroom or the parent has concerns pertaining to the student's current IEP.

The new teacher must remember that the parents are the true "experts" with regard to the student and often have beneficial information pertaining to strategies that have historically "worked" or "not worked" with the student. Parents should be viewed as consultants and valuable members of the student's educational team. The teacher should provide the parents with all information or documents pertaining to the meeting prior to the conference date. Parents must prepare for conferences in the same manner as the teacher to maximize the benefits of a school conference. Resource 6.2 provides information for parents in need of assistance in conference preparation.

FORM 6.1   Essential Tasks for All Parent–Teacher Conferences

Preconference Tasks

_____ Prior written notification of meeting should be given to the parents or guardian and other conference participants (At least 7 to 10 working days in advance).

_____ Conference notification should include the following (see Form 6.2):

    a.   Date, time, and exact location of conference

    b.   Purpose of conference

    c.   List of people and their respective positions to attend conference (include student's name on the notification; it is mandatory that a student of any age who has a disability be invited if the purpose of the meeting is to consider or discuss transition services).

    d   Request confirmation of attendance from all invitees. List special education teacher's name and telephone number as contact person for all conference inquiries.

_____ Select and reserve conference location. This location needs to be a neutral area that is comfortable and free from interruptions, such as the school's main conference room or the media center's conference room.

_____ Formulate a meeting agenda and distribute to parents or guardians and all school personnel invited to conference well in advance of the designated meeting date (letter or e-mail).

_____ Send parents or guardians a conference preparation handout (see Resource 6.2) prior to meeting.

_____ Telephone or e-mail parents or guardians 2 days prior to conference as a friendly reminder.

_____ Confirm conference with school personnel 2 days prior to conference through e-mail or letter (see Form 6.4).

_____ Ensure the following school personnel have been invited to the following conferences:

    a.   Progress Report Conference: parents or guardians, student (if appropriate), school administrator, general education teachers of included students, school counselor, special education teacher and additional special education staff.

(Continued)

FORM 6.1   Essential Tasks for All Parent–Teacher Conferences

b. Problem-Solving Conference: parents or guardians, student (if appropriate), school administrator, general education teachers of included students, school counselor, special education coordinator or support person, special education teacher or special education staff.

c. IEP Conference: parents or guardians, at least one general education teacher of included students, at least one special education teacher, school or special education administrator, related services provider, transition service participants, and the student (if appropriate).

Conference Tasks

_____ Introduce school principal, faculty, and special education personnel to parents or guardians.

_____ Give parents' legal rights booklet to the parents or guardians when appropriate.

_____ State the purpose of the conference.

_____ The special education teacher should appoint an individual to take copious notes during the meeting and highlight all significant information in the minutes of the meeting.

_____ The special education teacher should close the conference by summarizing all information discussed and review any additions to the student's IEP.

_____ All information discussed and plans developed during the meeting should be written on minutes form and signed by all people attending the conference (see Form 6.6).

_____ Give parents or guardians a copy of the conference minutes.

Postconference Tasks

_____ Send parents or guardians a summary of the meeting in a letter format and include the following (see Form 6.7):

a. Thank parents for attending the meeting.

b. Send any documents requested by the parents during the meeting.

c. Indicate the best school hours and days to reach the special education teacher if parents have further questions.

d. Conclude letter with positive comment about the student.

FORM 6.2   Essential Information for the Progress Report Conference

Directions: The following information must be collected and reviewed by the special education teacher prior to the progress report conference. All collected documentation should be shared with the parents or guardians in advance of the scheduled meeting.

Student Information

_____ Current student school attendance record:

a. Request a copy of the student's attendance record from your school's attendance office.

b. Review the student's tardy record and check-out early record.

c. Request that all teachers of included students note attendance and tardy information on the student's monitor form (see Chapter 3).

_____ Current student school discipline record:

a. Request a summary report of the student's discipline record from the school's discipline office or the student's discipline administrator.

b. Review the student's discipline record for the following:

1. Description of discipline referrals or classroom infractions or both

2. Discipline referrals date and time

3. Name of referring school official

_____ Review student's academic school record with the school counselor:

a. Review previous academic achievements.

b. Review student's academic portfolio.

c. Review the total number of earned high school units or credits.

d. Review the program of study or academic emphasis the student has decided to pursue.

Classroom Information

_____ Review the following information from general education teachers for students in inclusive settings:

___Class participation	___Class/daily work	___Portfolio
___Test grades	___On-task behavior	___Overall performance
___Quiz grades	___Tardy/absent	

Classroom Information

_____ Review information from special education teacher:

____ Current mastery of IEP goals and objectives

____ Current successful instructional strategies

____ Current successful behavior modification strategies

____ Status on previously developed plans or strategies

____ Overall performance in the special education classroom

FORM 6.3   Essential Information for the Problem-Solving Conference

Directions: The following information must be collected and reviewed by the special education teacher prior to the problem-solving conference. All collected documentation should be shared with the parents in advance of the scheduled meeting.

A. IDENTIFY PRESENTING BEHAVIOR PROBLEM:

Problem involves:

1. Student self-control

2. Student affect: enthusiasm, leadership, followership, responsibility, reactions to rewards and contingencies.

3. Social conventions: manners, courtesy, respect for others and their property.

Problem occurs:

1. Special education classroom

2. General education classroom

3. Recess

4. Fieldtrips

5. School bus

6. Bathroom

7. Hallway

8. Cafeteria

B. IDENTIFY PRESENTING ACADEMIC PROBLEM:

Problem involves:

1. Student's performance in the area or areas of reading, spelling, English, science, social studies, math, or other

2. Student's performance on tests

3. Student's performance on quizzes

4. Student's homework completion

5. Student's completion of assigned projects

Problem occurs:

1. General education classroom or setting

   Class: _____   Teacher: _____

2. Special education classroom or setting

   Class: _____   Teacher: _____

FORM 6.4   Conference Notification

Date: _____

Student Name: _____   **Grade:** _____

Conference date and time: _____

Location: _____

Conference participants: (name and position)

_____   _____

_____   _____

_____   _____

_____   _____

Conference purpose:

_____

_____

_____

_____

Requested Information:

_____ Attendance   _____ Test grades

_____ Tardy   _____ Quiz grades

_____ Discipline   _____ On-task behavior

_____ Other:_____

_____

FORM 6.5   Conference Reminder

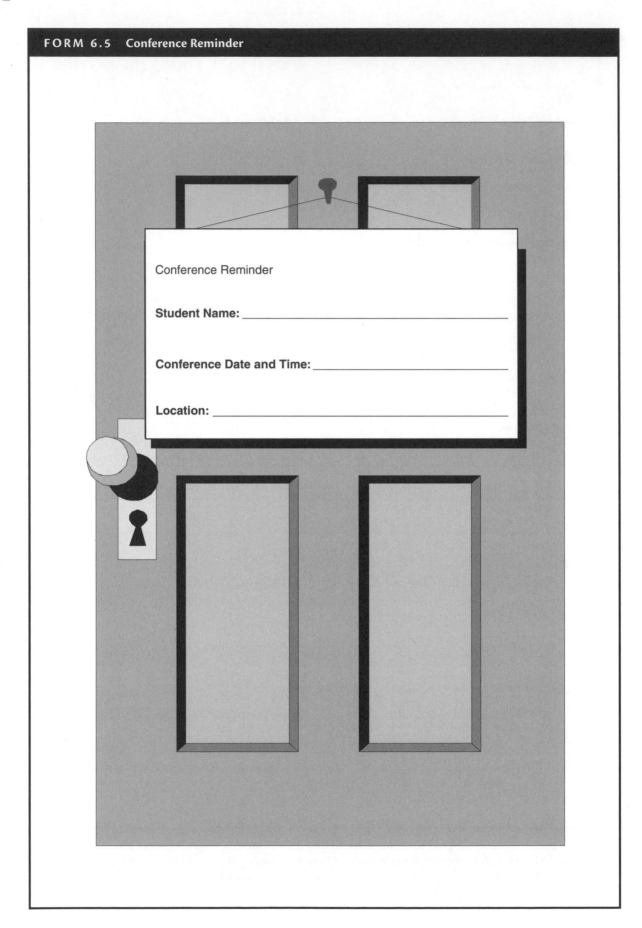

Conference Reminder

Student Name: _____

Conference Date and Time: _____

Location: _____

FORM 6.6   Conference Minutes

Date: _____

Student name: _____ Grade: _____

Current placement: _____

Conference purpose:

_____
_____
_____
_____

Conference summary:

_____
_____
_____
_____
_____
_____
_____
_____

Conference participants' signatures:

_____   _____

_____   _____

_____   _____

_____   _____

FORM 6.7 Conference Summary

Date:_____

Dear _____,

_____

_____

_____

_____

_____

_____

_____

_____

_____

_____

_____

_____

Sincerely,

Enclosures

_____ Meeting minutes   _____ Academic strategies

_____ IEP documents   _____ Behavior

_____ Behavior contracts   _____ Other

RESOURCE 6.1   Teacher Guidelines for Parent Conferences

Conference Dos:

- Be positive and personal.

- Show that you care.

- Be a good listener and watch the time.

- Use examples of children's work.

- Give and take suggestions.

- Have a specialist on hand if needed.

Conference Don'ts:

- Don't be defensive when parents ask about the classroom.

- Don't let a conference become confrontational.

- Don't surprise parents.

- Don't forget the "A" students.

- Don't use jargon.

RESOURCE 6.2   Parent Tips for Conference Preparation

Before the Conference:

- Make arrangements for your other children, if necessary. The conference is for you and your child's teacher; small children can be districting and take time away from the discussion.

- Jot down any questions you may have for the teacher, such as
  - Is my child working to the best of his (or her) ability?
  - How is he (or she) progressing in reading, math, handwriting, and other subjects?
  - Does he (or she) get along well with teachers, children?
  - Does he (or she) follow classroom rules?
  - What are his (or her) attitudes in class?
  - How do you handle (specific behavior)?
  - What do the tests say about his (or her) ability?

- Talk to your child about the conference. Ask if he or she wants you to ask any questions or voice any concerns.

- Collect any records or information that may help the teacher. Try to anticipate questions and prepare answers.

At the Conference:

- Please be on time and stay only for your scheduled time. You may schedule another conference if you do not cover all the necessary information in the allotted time.

- Discuss only the child at issue. Try not to stray off the subject. Do not bring up your other children's problems.

- Ask any questions about your child's education. Advocate for your child. Know your child's rights.

- Volunteer information that may help the teacher plan programming for your child.

- Feel free to take notes to review later.

After the Conference:

- Feel free to contact your child's teacher for further clarification.

Source: Adapted from Shea and Bauer (1991, p. 146).

RESOURCE 6.3   Dealing With the Anger of Parents

1. Have someone else present (teacher, administration, etc.)

2. Offer them a seat in a private setting—get off your feet

3. Wait and listen

4. Do not become defensive—tone of voice

5. Speak softly, slowly, remain calm and be aware of your posture

6. Show genuine interest in the student—express this

7. Do not fear anger—understand its origins

8. Try to determine the cause of the anger

9. Sometimes suggest a later meeting time

10. Use phrases that are placating

11. Not all parents are going to leave feeling good

12. Acknowledge their anger—convey concern

13. Avoid using angry responses, sarcasm, or negative nonverbal clues

14. Seek assistance or support from principal or counselor

Placating Responses

- "I feel uncomfortable discussing this now. Could we set up a time we could meet that would be convenient?"

- "I can appreciate how frustrating . . ."

- "We are here to help your child, and have only his best interest at heart."

- "Let me see if I understand what you are concerned about."

- "What do you want me to do? How do you want me to accomplish this?" Follow with

- "What can we do together?"

Source: Morehead (2001). Used with permission.

Understanding Educational Assessments

7

The desire to know is far more important than achievement and/or performance measures.

—G. Caine and R. Caine

The beginning special education teacher will administer a variety of educational assessments during the course of his or her career. The teacher should become familiar with the most common assessments that are administered not only to students with disabilities but also to all students due to the new requirements of the No Child Left Behind Act of 2001 (NCLB). NCLB was signed into law on January 8, 2002, and is built on four principles: accountability for results, more choices for parents, greater local control and flexibility, and an emphasis on doing what works based on scientific research. In that same vein, the Individuals with Disabilities Education Improvement Act of 2004 (U.S. Department of Education, 2004) also calls for "improving the outcomes for all students by using scientifically based instructional practices" (Cummings, Allison, Atkins, & Cole, 2008, p. 24). Traditionally, the expectation has been that new teachers are to have basic knowledge of the educational assessments used to screen, identify, place, and plan programs for students with disabilities; however, teachers must now be well versed in formative assessments that specifically measure student progress after receiving scientific, researched-based interventions. The process of identifying a student's need for support, implementing scientific researched-based interventions, and progress monitoring skill improvement or mastery through assessments is referred to as *response to intervention* (RTI). RTI is a process or model that must also be used for the purpose of determining a student's eligibility for special education services and during the evaluation process. NCLB and IDEA have both placed a new emphasis on using educational assessments as an accountability measure. The expectation under NCLB is that students with disabilities will achieve at the same level as nondisabled students. Thurlow, Elliott, and Ysseldyke (1998) state,

The reauthorization of the Individuals with Disabilities Education Act (IDEA), which funds special education programs, also requires that states report on the participation of students with disabilities in their state assessment programs and that an alternate assessment be used for those students who cannot be included in the statewide assessment program. (p. 7)

In light of this information, the number of students with disabilities taking high-stakes tests is on the rise across the nation, and the special education teacher along with the individualized education program (IEP) team is ultimately responsible for designing or selecting appropriate accommodations that will enable students with disabilities to participate in the same assessment process as students in the general education setting. The new teacher must possess a working knowledge of the assessments most commonly used in his or her school system and the acceptable or allowable accommodations for those assessments. The beginning teacher must also be proficient in the administration of educational assessments and the interpretation of students' tests results for the purpose of measuring student progress, program planning, instructional decision making, and accurately conveying all information to parents.

In Chapter 7, the authors provide the reader with four strategies that are designed to reacquaint the beginning teacher with basic test and measurement information; to increase his or her overall knowledge of the levels of educational assessments; to assist the new teacher in obtaining a clear understanding of the IDEA 2004 rules and regulations governing assessments for students with disabilities; to provide a brief overview of common accommodations for assessments; and to increase the beginning teacher's understanding of alternate assessments. The authors encourage the teacher to review his or her district's policies and procedures pertaining to student assessments before administering any tests and releasing student results. After reviewing the information in this chapter, the new teacher should be able to administer and interpret educational assessments with precision and confidence.

SECTION 1: REVIEW BASIC TEST AND MEASUREMENT INFORMATION

Standardized Tests

These tests are commercially prepared by experts in measurement and subject matter. They provide methods for obtaining samples of behavior under uniform procedures, and scoring is usually objective. Typically, a standardized test has been administered to a norm group (or groups) so that a person's performance can be interpreted by comparing it to the performance of others—that is, the test is norm-referenced (Merhrens & Lehmann, 1987, pp. 7–8).

Test Classifications

A. Cognitive measures: These are measures of maximum performance (how well a person will do when motivated to obtain as high a score as possible).

1. Aptitude tests: These tests are designed to predict success in some future learning activity.

2. Achievement tests: These tests are designed to indicate the degree of success in some past learning activity.

B. Noncognitive measures: These are measures of typical behavior (procedures of this type are concerned with what the individual will do rather than what he or she can do).

1. Interest inventories

2. Personality inventories

3. Attitude inventories

Test Characteristics

The following is a list of components that are essential when determining the adequacy of any assessment (formal or informal):

A. Reliability: This refers to the consistency and stability of assessment results.

B. Validity: This refers to the meaningfulness and appropriateness of the uses and interpretations to be made of assessment results. Validity is the most significant aspect of any test.

C. Normative information: A comparison can be made of one student's results to those of other students who have taken the same test. According to Linn and Gronlund (1995), there are four basic types of test norms:

1. Grade norms (grade equivalents): Grade group in which student's raw score is average. Note: Grade equivalents should never be interpreted literally; at best, they are only a rough guide as to the level of test performance.

2. Percentile norms (percentile ranks or percentile scores): Percentage of students in the reference group who fall below student's raw score.

3. Standard-score norms (standard scores): Distance of student's raw score above or below the mean of the reference group in terms of standard deviation units. (p. 444)

4. Stanines: Stanines are essentially groups of percentile ranks, with the entire group of scores divided into nine parts, with the largest number of individuals falling in the middle stanines and fewer students falling at the extremes. Few tests in common usage use stanines today, although these scores can be useful in understanding the relative range of a student's performance (Canter, 1998, p. 119).

Note: The teacher should always check the latest copyright date to ensure that the norms have been updated in an effort to keep the test current.

Test Interpretation

A. Norm-Referenced Interpretation: Describes the performance in terms of the relative position held in some known group. Individual scores are compared to standard or group scores. A norm-referenced test is designed to provide a measure of performance that is interpretable in terms of an individual's relative standing in some known group.

Example: Jane typed better than 85 percent of the class members.

B. Criterion-Referenced Interpretation: Describes the specific performance that was demonstrated. The criterion-referenced test is designed to provide a measure of performance that is interpretable in terms of a clearly defined and delimited domain of learning task.

Example: Jane typed 40 words per minute without error.

SECTION 2: UNDERSTAND THE LEVELS OF EDUCATIONAL ASSESSMENTS IN SCHOOLS

Educational assessments serve as tools to collect information pertaining to a student's performance in the school setting. Students with disabilities typically undergo a variety of educational assessments at various levels prior to being placed in a designated special education program or setting. The first level of assessment usually begins in the general education classroom where the teacher identifies a student who consistently fails to perform academically or exhibits frequent inappropriate behavior. The special education teacher can be asked to review a student's work samples or complete a classroom observation. The new special education teacher should be able to determine if there is a sufficient amount of evidence to refer the student for diagnostic testing. Diagnostic testing is usually the second level of educational assessment. The school counselor or special education teacher can be responsible for specific diagnostic testing at the school level. The student should be referred to the third assessment level if the diagnostic assessments continue to identify deficit or problem areas. At the third level, a licensed school psychologist usually conducts a comprehensive educational assessment. A battery of tests is administered to the student in order to measure the student's intellectual aptitudes, academic achievement, acuity, and learning style. In addition, classroom observations are conducted to document how the student functions academically, behaviorally, and socially in the classroom. Student work samples are collected from the classroom teacher. An adaptive behavior scale is usually completed if the student is suspected of being intellectually disabled. For initial referrals, the parents complete an in-depth developmental and medical history and the student's permanent school record is reviewed. The school psychologist compiles all test results (formal and informal), observations, work samples, and parent and school history information and completes the final assessment report. The report is presented to a team of educators, the student's parents, and the student (when appropriate) and the results are explained and discussed at great length. This report is the basis for student placement and the development of an individualized educational program.

SECTION 3: KNOW THE CURRENT IDEA RULES AND REGULATIONS PERTAINING TO ASSESSING STUDENTS WITH DISABILITIES

The special education teacher must know and understand the rules and regulations that pertain to the assessment of students with disabilities. In Section 300.320, titled, "Definition of Individualized Education Program," the federal guidelines pertaining to appropriate accommodations and alternate assessments are listed as follows:

> (6)(i) A statement of any individual appropriate accommodations that are necessary to measure the academic achievement and functional performance of the child on State and districtwide assessments consistent with section 612(a)(16) of the Act; and

> (6)(ii) If the IEP Team determines that the child must take an alternate assessment instead of a particular regular State or districtwide assessment of student achievement, a statement of why—

>> (A) The child cannot participate in the regular assessment;

>> (B) The particular alternate assessment selected is appropriate for the child.

SECTION 4: REVIEW OF ALTERNATE ASSESSMENTS

Alternate assessments are instruments designed to obtain information pertaining to student performance. Browder et al. (2004) state, "Although not limited to this population, most students with severe disabilities (severe cognitive disabilities, multiple disabilities, severe autism, deaf-blindness) require an alternate assessment" (p. 211). According to federal legislation, all states are required to have alternate assessments for students with disabilities who cannot take a grade-level assessment. Alternate assessments must

> (a) address the unique needs of a small but heterogeneous population of students unable to participate in general assessments; (b) align to the general curriculum in reading, language arts, math, and science; (c) adhere to standards of technical adequacy; and (d) be instructionally relevant for teachers and students. (Johnson & Arnold, 2007, p. 24)

There are many different approaches and formats of alternate assessments. Roeber (2002) has identified and defined the types of alternate assessments:

Checklists.

This method relies on teachers to remember whether students are able to carry out certain activities. This technique has the advantage of permitting the rapid collection of information, but due to the nature of the observation, may not be highly reliable. Scores reported are usually the number of skills that the student was able to successfully perform. This method will permit the scores of students to be added up and reported.

Observation in Structured and Unstructured Settings.

This assessment method encourages teachers, after training, to observe whether students are able to perform certain activities. Observation in unstructured situations is on-going observation of the student in everyday classroom and other settings, without any overt attempt to increase the likelihood that the skill will occur. By setting up structured situations, the teachers [are] setting up a structure in which the skill being observed is more likely to occur, thus making the observation of it more likely. Scores reported are usually the number of skills that the student was able to successfully perform. This method will permit the scores of students to be added up and reported.

Performance Assessments.

These assessments are direct measures of the skill, usually in a one-on-one assessment. Due to the nature of students' disabilities, rarely are these paper-based assessments. More likely, the teacher and the student work through an assessment that uses manipulatives, and the teacher observes whether students are able to perform the assigned tasks. Such assessments have the disadvantage of being time-intensive, so that an assessment may be limited to only a handful of skills. Scores are typically assigned to each performance assessment, although in more complex performance assessments, there is an underlying scale of task complexity that may form the basis for reporting.

Samples of Student Work.

Students may in the course of learning produce samples of work that demonstrate the skills being assessed. These "artifacts" can be assessed. While this assessment method has the advantage of using existing work in the assessment process, not all students will be able to produce samples, and even for those who do, it may not be possible to determine how much of the work is that of the student. Scores are assigned to each piece of work.

Portfolios.

This assessment method uses a collection of student work, performance assessments, observations, and other data about students to judge student achievement. Usually, the various pieces collected to demonstrate the performance on each standard or group of standards are judged together, although occasionally, the entire content area or entire portfolio may be assigned a single score.

Source: Roeber, E. (2002). *Setting standards on alternate assessments* (Synthesis Report 42). Minneapolis, MN: University of Minnesota, National Center on Educational Outcomes. Retrieved April 26, 2008, from the World Wide Web: http://education.umn.edu/NCEO/OnlinePubs/Synthesis42.html.

SECTION 5: REVIEW OF APPROPRIATE ASSESSMENT ACCOMMODATIONS

The special education teacher in conjunction with the IEP team is responsible for determining if a student with a disability will participate in state or district-wide testing. In most states, the IEP team also determines the need for a student to receive accommodations when taking an educational assessment. In *Testing Students With Disabilities*, Thurlow and colleagues (1998) define accommodations as "changes in testing materials or procedures that enable the student with disabilities to participate in an assessment in a way that allows abilities to be assessed rather than disabilities" (pp. 27–28). In addition, the authors of the same text have identified the following types of accommodations:

- Setting accommodations
- Timing accommodations
- Scheduling accommodations
- Presentation accommodations
- Response accommodations
- Other accommodations (out-of-level testing, motivational accommodations, and test preparation)

All selected accommodations must parallel those regularly provided to the student with disabilities in the general or special education classroom.

FORM 7.1 Test Administration Checklist

The following checklist will guide the new special education teacher through his or her first test administration. The checklist is divided into three main sections. Space is provided for the teacher to add additional items to each section.

Prior to Test

_____Send parents notification of test date and time. Request parents' permission as directed by school system policy.

_____Inform the student or students in advance of the upcoming test date.

_____Thoroughly read the examiner's manual of the test to be administered.

_____Check and assemble all test materials. Test materials could possibly include:

- #2 pencils
- Stopwatch
- Student booklets
- Examiner's manual
- Scratch paper
- Calculators
- Testing—Do Not Disturb Sign

_____Select and reserve testing location. The test location should be comfortable and free of distractions.

_____Review the examiner's manual the day before testing and highlight important notes or items in the directions. In addition, colored adhesive tabs can be placed in the examiner's manual to mark each section of the test.

_____Other:_____

During the Test

_____Post the _Testing—Do Not Disturb_ sign on the outside of the door of test location.

_____Request students to sign in if testing in a large group.

_____Distribute test materials to student.

_____Read the test directions to students.

_____Write the start time of the test in a highly visible location when testing in a large group.

_____Monitor students.

_____Other:_____

After the Test

_____Collect all test materials carefully and promptly.

_____Collect pencils, scratch paper, or other materials given to student or students for testing purposes.

_____Remove testing sign from door.

_____Return to classroom and count test materials.

_____Place order to replenish test materials.

_____Store all tests in a secure location until they can be sent for scoring or the teacher arranges to score the test.

_____Write formal report on test results.

_____Other:_____

RESOURCE 7.1   Educational Assessments

The following is an overview of various assessments the first-year special education teacher may encounter at ysome point during his or her career. Some of the tests listed below are utilized in identifying students with disabilities while others can be utilized to measure student progress. The list is only a sampling of the multitude of assessments that are in existence.

AAMR Adaptive Behavior Scale-School, Second Edition

Authors: Nadine Lambert, Kazuo Nihira, and Henry Leland

Purpose: "Used to assess adaptive behavior."

Bender Visual Motor Gestalt Test, Second Edition

Author: Lauretta Bender

Age Group: All ages

Purpose: "Assess the visual—motor functions of individuals from age three years to adulthood. Also used in the evaluation of developmental problems in children, learning disabilities, retardation, psychosis, and organic brain disorders." (p. 37)

California Achievement Tests, Fifth Edition

Author: CTB Macmillan/McGraw-Hill

Purpose: "Designed to measure achievement in the basic skills taught in schools throughout the nation."

Criterion Test of Basic Skills [2000 Edition]

Authors: Keith Lundell, William Brown, and James Evans

Purpose: "Developed to assess the basic reading and arithmetic skills of individual students."

Differential Aptitude Tests, Fifth Edition

Authors: G. K. Bennett, H. G. Seashore, and A. G. Wesman

Purpose: "Designed to measure students' ability to learn or to succeed in a number of different areas."

*House-Tree-Person and Draw-A-Person as Measure of Abuse in Children: A Quantitative Scoring System

Author: Valerie Van Hutton

Purpose: "Developed to assess personality/emotional characteristics of sexually abused children."

*Iowa Tests of Basic Skills(r), Forms K, L, and M

Author: H. D. Hoover, A. N. Hieronymous, D. A. Frisbie, and S. B. Dunbar

Purpose: "To provide a comprehensive assessment of student progress in the basic skills."

The Minnesota Multiphasic Personality Inventory–2

Authors: James N. Butcher, W. Grant Dahlstrom, John R. Graham, Auke Tellegen, and Beverly Kaemmer

Purpose: "Designed to assess a number of the major patterns of personality and emotional disorders."

Otis–Lennon School Ability Test, Seventh Edition

Authors: Arthur S. Otis and Roger T. Lennon

Purpose: "Designed to measure abstract thinking and reasoning ability."

Peabody Individual Achievement Test–Revised [1998 Normative Update]

Author: Frederick C. Markwardt Jr.

Purpose: "Designed to measure academic achievement."

(Continued)

RESOURCE 7.1   (Continued)

Peabody Picture Vocabulary Test–III

Authors: Lloyd M. Dunn, Leota M. Dunn, Kathleen T. Williams, and Jing-Jen Wang.

Purpose: "Designed to measure receptive vocabulary and can also be used as a screening test of verbal ability."

Rotter Incomplete Sentences Blank, Second Edition

Authors: Julian B. Rotter, Michael I. Lah, and Janet E. Rafferty

Purpose: Primarily used "as a screening instrument of overall adjustment."

Scales for Diagnosing Attention-Deficit/Hyperactivity Disorder

Authors: Gail Ryser and Kathleen McConnell

Purpose: "To help identify children and adolescents who have attention deficit/hyperactivity disorder (ADHD)."

Stanford-Binet Intelligence Scale, Fourth Edition

Authors: Robert L. Thorndike, Elizabeth P. Hagen, Jerome M. Sattler, Elizabeth A. Delaney, and Thomas F. Hopkins.

Purpose: Designed as "an instrument for measuring cognitive abilities that provides an analysis of pattern as well as the overall level of an individual's cognitive development."

Test of Nonverbal Intelligence, Third Edition

Authors: Linda Brown, Rita J. Sherbenou, and Susan K. Johnsen

Purpose: "Developed to assess aptitude, intelligence, abstract reasoning, and problem solving in a completely language-free format."

Test of Written Language–Third Edition

Authors: Donald D. Hammill and Stephen C. Larsen

Purpose: Designed to "(a) identify students who perform significantly more poorly than their peers in writing and who as a result need special help; (b) determine a student's particular strengths and weaknesses in various writing abilities; (c) document a student's progress in a special writing program; and conduct research in writing."

Vineland Adaptive Behavior Scales

Authors: Sara S. Sparrow, David A. Balla, Domenic V. Cicchetti, and Patti L. Harrison.

Purpose: To "assess personal and social sufficiency of individuals from birth to adulthood."

Wechsler Intelligence Scale for Children–Third Edition

Author: David Wechsler

Purpose: A "measure of a child's intellectual ability."

Wide Range Achievement Test 3

Author: Gary S. Wilkinson

Purpose: To measure the skills needed to learn reading, spelling, and arithmetic.

Sources: Buros Institute of Mental Measurement Test Reviews Online. (n.d.). Retrieved April 23, 2004, from http://buros.unl.edu/buros/jsp/reviews.jsp?item=06000003.

Sweetland, R. C., & O'Connor, W. (Eds.). (1984). *Tests: A comprehensive reference for assessments in psychology, education and business.* Kansas City, MO: SKS Associates.

RESOURCE 7.2   Possible Accommodations for Students With Disabilities

The Florida Department of Education has identified the following possible accommodations for IEP teams to consider for students with disabilities. The reader should use the information as only guide when developing appropriate accommodations for individual students.

- **Flexible Setting**

   Students may take an assessment individually or in a small group setting under a proctor's supervision. Lighting, acoustics, adaptive or special furniture, and distraction-free locations, are flexible setting situations for consideration.

- **Flexible Scheduling**

   Students may take the test during several brief sessions within one school day. More frequent or extended breaks may be needed. The test may be administered at a time of day that is most beneficial to the student. Test proctors may need to encourage students to answer one type of test question first and then others (e.g., multiple choice may be easier for a particular student than extended response questions).

- **Flexible Timing**

   Students may be provided additional time. Caution should be taken in automatically providing extended time. Test proctors should carefully monitor the use of time by students. Extended testing time may only prolong test anxiety for some students; test proctors should be attuned to the needs of each student using modifications. Students who are testing with Braille or large print versions generally benefit from the use of extended time because of the reduced reading speed typically associated with the use of these formats.

- **Flexible Presentation**

   Students may use mechanical aids such as a magnifying device, a pointer, a template, or other similar device to assist in maintaining visual attention to the test items. Directions and items not assessing reading may be read to students. Directions may be reread, paraphrased, or simplified. It may be helpful for students to restate the directions in their own words. Test proctors may need to color code the instructions to help emphasize the steps. Other presentation considerations include reading or signing directions, writing prompts, or math items to students; turning the pages for the student; allowing the teacher who typically works with the student to administer the test; assisting the student with moving from one item to another; and encouragement by test proctor to begin, keep going, or stay on task without affecting the student's choice of responses on the test.

- **Flexible Responding**

   Students may provide an oral response, a signed response, a response on a word processor, or a response on a Braille writer. If an oral response is given by a student on the Florida Writing Assessment, the student must indicate punctuation. Directions for transcribing oral, signed, or word-processed responses are indicated in the testing instructions available from the district test coordinator. Student responses must not be edited when transcribed. Other flexible responding considerations include allowing the student to write in the test booklet or allowing the student to use special paper (lined or gridded).

Source: Technical Assistance Paper, Florida Department of Education, Division of Public Schools and Community Education, Bureau of Instructional Support and Community Services (July 1998).

RESOURCE 7.3 **Formative and Summative Assessments**

- *Formative assessments* are on-going assessments, reviews, and observations in a classroom. Teachers use formative assessment to improve instructional methods and student feedback throughout the teaching and learning process. For example, if a teacher observes that some students do not grasp a concept, she or he can design a review activity or use a different instructional strategy. Likewise, students can monitor their progress with periodic quizzes and performance tasks. The results of formative assessments are used to modify and validate instruction.

    Examples:

    a. Anecdotal records
    b. Quizzes and essays
    c. Diagnostic tests

- *Summative assessments* are typically used to evaluate the effectiveness of instructional programs and services at the end of an academic year or at a pre-determined time. The goal of summative assessments is to make a judgment of student competency—after an instructional phase is complete. For example, in Florida, the FCAT is administered once a year—it is a summative assessment to determine each student's ability at pre-determined points in time. Summative evaluations are used to determine if students have mastered specific competencies and to identify instructional areas that need additional attention.

    Examples:

    a. Final exams
    b. CRCT
    c. SAT and ACT

Source: Classroom Assessment. (n.d.). Retrieved April 21, 2008, from http://fcit.usf.edu/assessment/basic/basica.html.

Writing a Legal and Effective Individualized Education Program

Good plans shape good decisions. That's why good planning helps to make elusive dreams come true.

—Lester R. Bittel

The writing of a legal and effective individualized education program (IEP) for a student with a disability is the most critical task the first-year special education teacher will undertake during the school year. The IEP is a legal document that is mandated by the Individuals with Disabilities Education Act (IDEA) and initially developed after the student is determined to be eligible for services. At a minimum, a team of individuals is required to meet, review, and revise the student's IEP annually and upon the completion of a reevaluation. The purpose of the annual meeting is to review the success of current instructional strategies, annotate the completion of current goals and objectives, and develop a solid plan designed to address the educational needs of the student. The IEP can be revised or revisited at any time, and the authors recommend that the special education teacher review the plan on a continuous basis throughout the year to chart student progress and to note significant problem areas. If the educational strategies, current placement, or any other factor in the plan appears to be ineffective, the teacher should organize a team meeting. The team must review all student information and make the appropriate adjustments to the student's IEP. According to the regulations, the IEP team must be composed of the parents of the child; not less than one general education teacher of the child if the child is currently participating in a general education class or possibly will at a future date; not less than one special education teacher of the child, or where appropriate, not less than one special education provider of the child; a school administrator or someone who has knowledge of general curriculum and resources; representatives of outside public agencies; and the student when deemed appropriate. Other individuals may participate as part of the IEP team at the parents' discretion. A tremendous amount of time and skill is involved in writing a plan that can meet the legal requirements or mandates and that effectively communicates the needs of the student. The plan serves as the instructional blueprint for special and general education teachers.

In this chapter, the authors provide the teacher with a summary and reference for each component. The authors focus on the content aspect of the IEP to assist the teacher in writing a plan that will survive a due process hearing. The authors have identified three basic skills that the special education teacher should possess before writing his or her first IEP. First, the new teacher must have a clear understanding of the IDEA rules and regulations that specifically address the content of the IEP. Next, the teacher must possess the ability to communicate all student information accurately and succinctly. The teacher should use language that can be easily understood by most audiences; provide information that is of an objective nature; and formulate an overall plan of action that can easily be followed by special and general education teachers, support personnel, and parents. The plan should be written on a personal level with positive overtones. Finally, the beginning teacher must establish and maintain rapport with parents and students to promote their active involvement in the IEP process. The authors provide the teacher with tips on how to increase the participation of students and parents and focus the importance of their roles in the development of a solid IEP. Parental support is critical to a student's success in the school setting. The chapter is structured in a format that will enlighten the teacher as to the legal aspects of the IEP and assist with writing of an effective plan. The authors have included an IEP conference summary form (see Form 8.1), information pertaining to the No Child Left Behind Act (see Resource 8.1), and a list of additional resource materials to assist with the writing of IEPs (see Resource 8.2). The authors encourage the reader to use only forms and documents that have been approved by his or her school system when conducting IEP meetings. In addition, the teacher must be familiar with his or her state laws that govern the education of students with disabilities.

SECTION 1: THE LEGAL REQUIREMENTS OF AN IEP

The first-year teacher must have a clear understanding of the current federal rules and regulations contained in the IDEA that specifically address the content of the IEP before attempting to write his or her first document. The essential information that every IEP is legally required to contain is specifically stated in Section 300.320 of the IDEA rules and regulations. The information in this section was obtained from the *Federal Register*, Volume 71, Number 156, August 14, 2008, Rules and Regulations. The authors strongly encourage the reader to obtain all updates of this information from his or her special education director or the U.S. Department of Education on a yearly basis.

Individualized Education Programs

§ 300.320 Definition of individualized education program.

(a) *General.* As used in this part, the term individualized education program or IEP means a written statement for each child with a disability that is developed, reviewed, and revised in a meeting in accordance with §§ 300.320 through 300.324, and that must include—

(1) A statement of the child's present levels of academic achievement and functional performance, including—

(i) How the child's disability affects the child's involvement and progress in the general education curriculum (i.e., the same curriculum as for nondisabled children); or

(ii) For preschool children, as appropriate, how the disability affects the child's participation in appropriate activities;

(2)(i) A statement of measurable annual goals, including academic and functional goals designed to—

(A) Meet the child's needs that result from the child's disability to enable the child to be involved in and make progress in the general education curriculum; and

(B) Meet each of the child's other educational needs that result from the child's disability;

(ii) For children with disabilities who take alternate assessments aligned to alternate achievement standards, a description of benchmarks or short-term objectives;

(3) A description of—

(i) How the child's progress toward meeting the annual goals described in paragraph (2) of this section will be measured; and

(ii) When periodic reports on the progress the child is making toward meeting the annual goals (such as through the use of quarterly or other periodic reports, concurrent with the issuance of report cards) will be provided;

(4) A statement of the special education and related services and supplementary aids and services, based on peer-reviewed research to the extent practicable, to be provided to the child, or on behalf of the child, and a statement of the program modifications or supports for school personnel that will be provided to enable the child—

(i) To advance appropriately toward attaining the annual goals;

(ii) To be involved in and make progress in the general education curriculum in accordance with paragraph (a)(1) of this section, and to participate in extracurricular and other nonacademic activities; and

(iii) To be educated and participate with other children with disabilities and nondisabled children in the activities described in this section;

(5) An explanation of the extent, if any, to which the child will not participate with nondisabled children in the regular class and in the activities described in paragraph (a)(4) of this section;

(Continued)

(Continued)

(6)(i) A statement of any individual appropriate accommodations that are necessary to measure the academic achievement and functional performance of the child on State and districtwide assessments consistent with section 612(a)(16) of the Act; and

   (ii) If the IEP Team determines that the child must take an alternate assessment instead of a particular regular State or districtwide assessment of student achievement, a statement of why—

     (A) The child cannot participate in the regular assessment; and

     (B) The particular alternate assessment selected is appropriate for the child; and

(7) The projected date for the beginning of the services and modifications described in paragraph (a)(4) of this section, and the anticipated frequency, location, and duration of those services and modifications.

(b) *Transition services.* Beginning not later than the first IEP to be in effect when the child turns 16, or younger if determined appropriate by the IEP Team, and updated annually, thereafter, the IEP must include—

(1) Appropriate measurable postsecondary goals based upon age appropriate transition assessments related to training, education, employment, and, where appropriate, independent living skills; and

(2) The transition services (including courses of study) needed to assist the child in reaching those goals.

(c) *Transfer of rights at age of majority.* Beginning not later than one year before the child reaches the age of majority under State law, the IEP must include a statement that the child has been informed of the child's rights under Part B of the Act, if any, that will transfer to the child on reaching the age of majority under § 300.520.

(d) *Construction.* Nothing in this section shall be construed to require—

(1) That additional information be included in a child's IEP beyond what is explicitly required in section 614 of the Act; or

(2) The IEP Team to include information under one component of a child's IEP that is already contained under another component of the child's IEP.

Source: 20 U.S.C. 1414(d)(1)(A) and (d)(6).

SECTION 2: UNDERSTANDING THE COMPONENTS OF AN IEP

Present Level of Performance

The authors view the present level of educational performance as one of the most important components of the IEP. In this section, an educational profile of the student is developed and reviewed with the IEP team. The profile should provide a comprehensive perspective of the student and lay the foundation on which to build the framework for the other IEP components. The present level of education performance is typically written in a narrative format and can be easily read by parents, students, and other professionals. The teacher is encouraged to write in nontechnical language and use the student's first name when appropriate. This will improve the readability and personalize the document. The authors consider the following information to be crucial to producing the present levels of educational performance component of the IEP. The special education teacher should write specific statements that address each area listed (as appropriate):

1. Current test/evaluation data

2. Vision and hearing screening

3. Student achievement

4. Communication skills

5. Strengths and weaknesses (e.g., reading comprehension and impulse control)

6. Social adaptation skills

7. Fine and gross motor skills

8. Psychomotor skills

9. Review of student progress in the special education classroom

10. Review of student progress in the general education classroom

Annual Goals and Objectives or Benchmarks

Annual goals are statements that address the student's areas of weakness that were identified in the present levels of performance section of the IEP. The goals should generally state what the student will be able to do by the end date of the IEP. For example,

1. Susan will be able to complete a simple job application form.

2. Susan will increase her reading comprehension skills.

An *objective* is a description of a performance one wants learners to be able to exhibit before one considers them competent. An objective describes an intended result of instruction rather than a process of instruction (Mager, 1984, p. 5). Objectives support the annual goals and must be measurable. A good objective will specifically state what the learner is to do, under what conditions the performance will occur, and the quality level of the performance. The special education teacher must progress monitor the student's objectives and make adjustments to instruction or instructional strategies to ensure student mastery. Remember that every objective must have a review date, method of evaluation, and criteria for mastery. For example,

1. Given the personal information section on a simple job application, the student will complete the section with less than five errors.

2. Given a selected story in the student's basal reader, the student will read the story silently and then answer four out of five comprehension questions correctly.

Services, Supplementary Aids, and Program Modifications or Supports

1. Special education services: State specific special education program and environment in which the student will be serviced.

2. Related services areas: occupational therapy, physical therapy, adaptive PE, special and regular transportation, counseling services, and so on.

Student Placement: Academic, Extracurricular, and Nonacademic Activities

1. Academic: core curriculum area, exploratory, specialty, or elective classes

2. Extracurricular: clubs, athletic teams, cheerleading, and so on

3. Nonacademic: lunch, recess, assemblies, and so on

Individual Accommodations for Student Achievement Assessments

Special education students must be assessed during the school year. The IEP team must state an alternative assessment method if the student is not going to participate in the statewide testing program. IDEA allows for reasonable test accommodations. Examples of acceptable test accommodations for standardized test are as follows:

1. Small group testing

2. Individual testing

3. Read test to student

4. Provide alternative response methods

5. Test in a room with carpet

6. Provide student with a study carrel

Service Dates, Frequency, Location, Duration, and Program Modifications

1. Specifically state the exact start and end dates of the IEP.

2. The IEP should list the school or facility location. Frequency and duration of service indicate how often and for how long the service is to be delivered.

3. Program modifications refer to the adaptations the teacher is implementing for the student to be successful in the classroom.

Student Progress: Measuring, Evaluating, Informing Parents, and Transition Services

1. Examples of measurement and evaluation tools are teacher-made tests, textbook unit tests, standardized tests, behavior rating scale, class point system, and teacher observation.

2. Informing parents: Parents should be informed via school report card, school progress report, weekly progress report, telephone, and parent-teacher conferences.

3. A transition plan must be developed for students age 14. A good transition plan will address the student's needs, interests, and aptitudes. Transition activities include community, daily living, and employment experiences. Transition plans should address high school programs of study and post-secondary options for older students.

SECTION 3: INVOLVING STUDENTS AND PARENTS IN THE IEP PROCESS

The involvement of students (at the appropriate age) and parents in the IEP process is mandated by IDEA; their active participation as team members is critical to the success of the IEP. The authors have found that the following strategies increase the active participation of parents in the IEP process:

1. Establish a working relationship or rapport with parents prior to any mandatory meetings.

2. Establish and maintain an open line of communication with parents throughout the school year.

3. Personally call to arrange the IEP meeting at a date and time convenient for the parents, and follow up with the required written notification.

4. The IEP meeting should be held in a location that is comfortable and free of distractions.

5. The seating arrangement should be in a manner that projects the feeling of equity among the team members (use a round table instead of a rectangle one).

6. Team members should use language throughout the conference that is simple and free of professional jargon.

7. Team members should listen to parent concerns or comments or both and encourage parents to be active participants throughout the conference.

8. Ensure that the parents leave the conference with an understanding of the plan for their child and confident that all plans will be carried out by all designated individuals.

9. Follow up with parents a few days after the meeting to check for any additional questions or concerns.

The new teacher will find that encouraging students who are of the appropriate age to become active participants in the process is a more challenging task. Older students are often unclear as to their current status and the entire IEP concept. The authors suggest involving the student in the planning of the IEP meeting date and discussing all information that will be reviewed during the time period. During their search for effective strategies to promote student involvement, the authors discovered the concept of "student-led IEPs." Mason, McGahee-Kovac, and Johnson (2004) found the following:

> Process-student-led IEPs teach students to take ownership for their own education and to demonstrate that ownership at an annual IEP meeting. Through our research on student-led IEPs, we found that students and teachers alike reported that students using this process knew more about their disabilities, legal rights, and appropriate accommodations than other students and that students gained increased self-confidence and the ability to advocate for themselves. (p. 18)

The student-led IEP has three levels of student involvement; the students receive training in the IEP process from the special education teacher. The culminating activity is when the student actually conducts the IEP conference. Although the authors are unclear as to the legal and ethical issues surrounding the concept, this is definitely an "out-of-the-box" idea and one worth a second look.

FORM 8.1   Essential Information for the Annual Individual Education Program Conference

Directions: The special education teacher must review his or her school district's policies regarding IEP conferences and use only approved special education forms for all formal IEP meetings. The following information must be collected and reviewed by the special education teacher prior to the annual IEP conference. All collected documentation should be shared with the parents in advance of the scheduled meeting.

_____**Review Current Levels of Performance**

1. Educational assessments

    a. Intelligence

    b. Academic achievement

    c. Learning style

    d. Adaptive behavior

    e. Social/emotional

    f. Fine and gross motor skills

2. Audiological assessment

3. Speech/language pathologist assessment

4. Physical therapy assessment

5. Occupational therapy assessment

6. Fine and gross motor skills assessment

7. Current medical status

_____**Review Current Individualized Education Program**

1. Goals and objectives (annotate the mastered goals and objectives on current IEP)

2. Related services: transportation, physical therapy, occupational therapy, speech and language therapy, other

3. Student's current placement

(Continued)

FORM 8.1 (Continued)

_____Regular class   _____Private separate school facility
_____Resource class   _____Public residential facility
_____Separate/self-contained class   _____Private residential facility
_____Public separate school facility   _____Homebound/hospital environment

4. Student's discipline plan

5. Student's behavior management plan

6. Student's standardized testing modifications

7. Student's transition plan

_____**Review Student's Performance in Regular Education Classes**

1. Test grades

2. Quiz grades

3. Academic portfolio

4. Homework completion

5. Class participation

6. On-task behavior

7. Conduct

_____**Review General Student Information**

1. Attendance record

2. Discipline record

3. School transcript (high school students only)

4. Student program of study (high school students only)

RESOURCE 8.1   Four Pillars of NCLB

Stronger Accountability for Results

Under *No Child Left Behind*, states are working to close the achievement gap and make sure all students, including those who are disadvantaged, achieve academic proficiency. Annual state and school district report cards inform parents and communities about state and school progress. Schools that do not make progress must provide supplemental services, such as free tutoring or after-school assistance; take corrective actions; and, if still not making adequate yearly progress after five years, make dramatic changes to the way the school is run.

More Freedom for States and Communities

Under *No Child Left Behind*, states and school districts have unprecedented flexibility in how they use federal education funds. For example, it is possible for most school districts to transfer up to 50 percent of the federal formula grant funds they receive under the Improving Teacher Quality State Grants, Educational Technology, Innovative Programs, and Safe and Drug-Free Schools programs to any one of these programs, or to their Title I program, without separate approval. This allows districts to use funds for their particular needs, such as hiring new teachers, increasing teacher pay, and improving teacher training and professional development.

Proven Education Methods

No Child Left Behind puts emphasis on determining which educational programs and practices have been proven effective through rigorous scientific research. Federal funding is targeted to support the programs and teaching methods that work to improve student learning and achievement. In reading, for example, *No Child Left Behind* supports scientifically based instruction programs in the early grades under the Reading First program and in preschool under the Early Reading First program.

More Choices for Parents

Parents of children in low-performing schools have new options under *No Child Left Behind*. In schools that do not meet state standards for at least two consecutive years, parents may transfer their children to a better-performing public school, including a public charter school, within their district. The district must provide transportation, using Title I funds if necessary. Students from low-income families in schools that fail to meet state standards for at least three years are eligible to receive supplemental educational services, including tutoring, after-school services, and summer school. Also, students who attend a persistently dangerous school or are the victim of a violent crime while in their school have the option to attend a safe school within their district.

Source: U.S. Department of Education (2004).

RESOURCE 8.2   IEP Reference Material

Better IEPs: How to Develop Legally Correct and Educationally Useful Programs
Barbara D. Bateman and Mary Anne Linden
Paperback; January 1, 2006

IEP and Inclusion TIPS for Parents and Teachers
Anne I. Eason and Kathy Whitbread
Spiral-bound; January 1, 2006

Successful Inclusion Strategies for Secondary and Middle School Teachers and IEP Pro CD-Rom Value-Pack
M. C. Gore and Lawrence E. Steel
Paperback; March 24, 2006

Transition IEPs: A Curriculum Guide for Teachers and Transition Practitioners
Paul Wehman
Hardcover; December 2008

Understanding, Developing, and Writing Effective IEPs: A Step-by-Step Guide for Educators
Roger Pierangelo and George A. Giuliani
Paperback; April 6, 2007

Writing Measurable IEP Goals and Objectives
Barbara Bateman
Paperback; January 1, 2006

Preparing Students for Transition

Every transition is an adventure—a challenge for growth and discovery.

—Steve Brunkhorst

The beginning special education teacher must prepare students for successful transition experiences. Although the authors agree with Steve Brunkhorst's view of transitions in terms of adventure, growth, and discovery, they have found that students with disabilities and their parents frequently approach transition experiences with a tremendous amount of trepidation. According to Kohler and Field (2003), "Transition to adult roles can be a complicated process, one that all youths must negotiate, and a myriad of factors work together to affect students' lives after school completion" (p. 181). Most people "transition" at approximately age 5 or 6 to public or private school; exit school at approximately age 18 to the post-school life options of work, marriage, college, or the military; and many retire at approximately age 62. Wehman (1996) has found that planning for transitions at all ages promotes the social and emotional well-being of students with disabilities. Planning for major life transitions, such as enrollment in full-day school and the change from school to post-school, is mandated by the Individuals with Disabilities Education Act (IDEA). Any change in a student's schedule, placement, school, or even transportation, however, should be viewed as an opportunity to help the student prepare for future transition experiences. The special education teacher, along with the individualized education program (IEP) team, is responsible for developing effective plans to prepare students for a variety of transitions ranging from changing schools to pursuing post-school endeavors. The role of the special education teacher is to provide students with strategies that will lay the foundation for successful transition experiences and to facilitate students' explorations of possibilities for post-school options and the setting of realistic career goals with each student's strengths, challenges, interests, and abilities in mind. The transition planning process provides an excellent opportunity to increase the self-advocacy and self-determination skills of students as they prepare for adulthood. Many students with disabilities have traditionally not been afforded the same number of opportunities to make decisions and choices as students without disabilities. Empowering students to be self-directed should be the ultimate goal of the special education teacher, and working with the student on transition planning can help to empower the student.

In this chapter, three strategies are presented that will assist the new teacher in his or her efforts to prepare students for transitions. The strategies involve providing an overview of the IDEA rules and regulations pertaining to the transition of students with disabilities and assisting students with two common transitional issues. These issues revolve around the movement of students with disabilities to a new school and to post-school experiences. The authors acknowledge that a tremendous amount of diversity exists among students with disabilities; the ultimate goal of the special education teacher must be to assist each student in developing the essential skills necessary to meet the challenges of independent living and to obtain employment in the modern workforce. Supplemental forms and resource information designed to assist the new teacher in preparing students for transitional experiences are provided at the end of the chapter.

STRATEGY 1: UNDERSTAND THE LEGAL ASPECTS OF TRANSITION

All IEPs of students age 14 or younger, when appropriate, must contain specific transition-related content. The IEPs of students age 16 and older must address transition services and include specific goals and objectives that focus on post-school outcomes. The transition component of the IEP must be reviewed annually. The student and any community agency personnel involved in transition planning, such as a vocational rehabilitation counselor, must be involved in the annual IEP meeting. In addition, the authors recommend that the school counselor be invited to the meeting. Scarborough and Gilbride (2006) state "it is important for school counselors to know that they are part of the team that is committed to keeping students with disabilities from 'slipping through the cracks'" (p. 11). The school counselor has a tremendous amount of resources and can function as another advocate for the student in the school environment.

The 2004 IDEA regulations pertaining to the IEP continue to include transition service needs (beginning at age 14 and updated annually) that focus on a student's course of study. This should include, when appropriate, the interagency responsibilities or needed linkages (beginning at age 16 or younger) and a statement that the child has been informed of the rights that will transfer to him or her on reaching the age of majority (CEC Today, 1999). For example, students planning to attend college should be informed of their rights to modifications in college or technical school classrooms under the Americans with Disabilities Act (ADA; Public Law 101–336). The reader should note that some school districts develop individual transition plans separately from the IEPs while others incorporate the transition plan into the student's IEP. Teachers should contact their local school district for specific guidelines.

STRATEGY 2: PREPARE STUDENTS FOR MOVEMENT TO A NEW SCHOOL

Changing schools can be a very traumatic event for students with disabilities. Going from elementary to middle school or middle to high school both involve several adjustments. For example, a child moving from a half-day preschool program to full-day first grade might need to prepare for navigating the lunchroom, playground, media center, or other new physical environments as well as classroom skills such as sitting in a desk, raising his or her hand to be called on, following instructions, taking turns, walking down the hall in line, and more. Students' concerns or issues vary depending on the grade level. Queen (2002) found that students moving from middle school to high school often have concerns pertaining to the following:

- Being tardy to class (getting to class on time), finding lockers, crowded hallways, and getting lost
- Being victimized and/or harassed by others
- Being safe at school
- Being able to understand difficult classes
- Coping with rigid rules and strict teachers
- Being able to make new friends in a new setting (p. 21)

Next, several suggestions to prepare students for positive transition experiences are discussed.

Suggestion 1: Conduct the Annual IEP Meeting at the New School

The IEP of each student is required to be reviewed on an annual basis. The authors suggest that the student's annual review meeting be held at the new school. This is a prime opportunity for the parents and student to meet the new special education teacher and ask the multitude of questions that typically accompany this type of transition. The meeting also provides the new teacher an opportunity to begin building rapport with the family, which is the key element to a successful partnership between home and school. In addition, the authors strongly urge the teachers from both schools to communicate on a regular basis to promote program continuity and maintain a clear understanding of the student expectations for the next level.

Suggestion 2: Create an Information Booklet

A primer or simple booklet providing useful information pertaining to the new school for students and parents given out well in advance of the change can be very helpful. Booklets may include information that is school specific, such as a school calendar, bell schedule, absence policy, dress code, code of conduct, extracurricular activities, and graduation requirements. The teacher may also use the booklet to provide information that is specific to his or her classroom or program and to highlight classroom policies and procedures, expectations, required student materials, and teacher contact information. The authors suggest including a list of the most common questions asked by parents and students and providing a response to each somewhere in the booklet.

Suggestion 3: Provide Private Orientation of the New School

Another helpful idea is for the parents and students to visit the new school to become familiar with the physical layout of the building. The orientation should include a school tour, an introduction to all special education and general education staff members the student will encounter during his or her school day, and an overview of important school policies and procedures. The authors recommend that the new teacher have the schedules of all students who will be served in general education settings available for students and parents to preview and find the locations of these classes. Also, the authors suggest that special education teachers of middle and high school students obtain all locker assignments for their students in advance and provide this information to students at the orientation. If the lockers have combination locks, students will need time to practice using the combinations to open their lockers. The inability to open a locker can be a source of stress for students at the middle and high school level. Finally, if the orientation session is offered during the day, this is a great opportunity for students and parents to meet other school staff members such as the principal, school counselor, secretaries, and custodians.

STRATEGY 3: PREPARE STUDENTS FOR POST-SCHOOL ENDEAVORS

The transition of students with disabilities to post-school experiences is typically filled with an array of emotions for students and parents. The time has finally arrived, and students must move to the next phase of their lives. The special education teacher must develop strategies designed to assist, facilitate, and promote the smooth transition of high school students to the next level of education or direct entry into the modern workforce. Students who plan to enter postsecondary institutions need assistance in setting goals, developing study and time management skills, achieving in high-level academic courses, and obtaining the academic skills necessary to become independent learners. Students who will enter directly into the modern workforce after high school need assistance in developing minimum entry-level skills in order to successfully gain employment. The authors present several suggestions to prepare students for post-school endeavors:

Suggestion 1: Focus on Career Development

The beginning teacher should integrate career development activities into his or her program or academic curriculum in order to promote career awareness and employment readiness skills with all students regardless of disability. The activities should be appropriate for the age and level of functioning of each student. The teacher should assist students in answering the following questions, which are critical to the career development process: Who am I? Where am I going? How am I going to get there? Next, the teacher should assist students in identifying their personal abilities, interests, and values in terms of work and then in developing a career goal that does not conflict with this information. Finally, the new teacher must assist students in acquiring the necessary knowledge and the application of skills that are necessary for achieving identified career goals. The authors encourage the beginning teacher to enlist the assistance of the school counselor when developing career activities for his or her students.

Suggestion 2: Assist Students in Meeting the Requirements for Admission to Postsecondary Institutions

According to Gil (2007), "As more students with disabilities enroll in institutions of higher education, it is essential that effective transition practices are in place" (p. 15). Students who have a desire to attend postsecondary institutions (technical colleges, two- and four-year colleges or universities) upon graduation from high school must possess the academic skills to gain entrance and survive in the higher-education environment. The special education teacher must ensure that the students on his or her caseload who plan to attend college are placed in high school programs of study that will prepare them for the rigor of college courses. The teacher should work closely with the school counselor to ensure that each student's course selections and standardized test scores meet the minimum requirements for his or her college selection. The authors have created a High School Four-Year Plan form (see Form 9.1) that the teacher can utilize to assist students and their parents in designing a high school plan that is appropriate for students pursuing a college education after graduation. The authors have also included a Unit of Credit Checklist form (see Form 9.2) that the teacher can use not only to monitor his or her students' progress toward meeting high school graduation requirements, but to ensure students are following their high school plan. Finally, students and parents typically have numerous questions as to the services that will be available to students with disabilities at the postsecondary institution. The U.S. Department of Education Office for Civil Rights (2002) has published a booklet that addresses these questions. The authors provide selections from the booklet at the end of the chapter so that the new teacher can assist parents in finding answers to their questions.

Materials or Resources

Form 9.1 High School Four-Year Plan

Form 9.2 Unit of Credit Checklist

Resource 9.1 Students With Disabilities Preparing for Postsecondary Education: Know Your Rights and Responsibilities

Suggestion 3: Focus on Work-Based Skills

The authors recommend that high school special education teachers working with students who are in the mild to moderate range of intellectual functioning develop an academic program that focuses on work-based skills. Typically, the students in this range of functioning are capable of acquiring the skills necessary to meet the challenges of independent living and working to some degree. The program should have a school-to-career focus and provide students with supervised work experiences designed to teach employability skills; gain job- or site-specific skills; foster work-oriented relationships with adults; and enable pupils to acquire attitudes, skills, and knowledge of life roles in real work settings. The teacher will find that despite his or her best efforts, there will be some students who require lifelong supervision; in keeping with the ultimate goal of transition, however, a work-based program will promote the skills necessary for independent living. The authors recommend several steps for developing a work-based education program for students with mild to moderate disabilities.

Step 1: Develop Program Goal

The primary goal of the work-based education program is to teach employability skills; gain job- or site-specific skills; foster work-oriented relationships with adults; and acquire the attitudes, skills, and knowledge for life roles in real work settings.

Step 2: Develop Program Objectives

The authors suggest that the reader select appropriate skill areas for his or her students and write instructional objectives in order to measure results. According to Mager (1984), "These statements are descriptions of intended results of instruction. They are descriptions of the standards we would like students to achieve or surpass" (p. 13). The information below is a list of School to Work units developed by Paula Bliss (2003), and contains the employability skills necessary for students to successfully enter the modern workforce. The authors encourage the new teacher to review the school to work units and develop student objectives.

1. About me/self-awareness: Students explore their interests, skills, abilities, values, learning styles, and occupational preferences through a variety of inventories and activities

2. Punctuality, attendance, and absenteeism

3. Personal appearance: dress, grooming, and personal cleanliness

4. Good worker character traits: dependability, honesty, positive attitude, willingness to work, how to deal with boredom at work

5. Communication skills: listening, speaking, reading, writing, nonverbal body language, sign language, and assertive communication

6. Getting along with supervisors

7. Getting along with coworkers

8. Income taxes and paycheck math

9. Job seeking skills: preparing a resume, filling out job applications forms, other job related forms and interviewing for a job

10. Money management

Source: Adapted from Paula Bliss, M.Ed., Special Education Teacher, http://www.paulabliss.com. Used with permission.

Step 3: Develop Guide for Program Implementation

The teacher must develop a step-by-step guide for implementing his or her work-based education program. The following steps are recommended for program implementation:

Meet with local businesses to secure job training sites for the school year.

Develop all necessary forms for the program.

    a. Business partner contract

    b. Parent permission

    c. Student commitment

Procure all materials needed to successfully implement the program.

Outline the vocational and employment skills to be addressed during the school year.

    a. Work performance at the job site

    b. Classroom performance on tests, quizzes, daily work, and projects

Develop program expectations for students.

    a. Dress code

    b. Classroom and job site behavior

Materials or Resources

Form 9.3 Work-Based Student Evaluation

Form 9.4 Student's Critique of Job Site

Resource 9.2 Work Behavior Training Strategies for Vocational Training for Students With Disabilities

Resource 9.3 Job Accommodations for People With Mental Retardation (MR) or Other Developmental Disabilities (DD)

FORM 9.1 High School Four-Year Plan

Name:_____ Graduation year:_____

Program of study (check):

_____College preparatory

_____Career technical preparatory

Area of concentration: _____

(Example of areas: agriculture, automotive, business, construction, culinary arts, graphic arts, technology)

_____Dual Seal (Both CP and CT)

Total units required for graduation: _____units

Subject Areas*	9th Grade	10th Grade	11th Grade	12th Grade
English				
Math				
Science				
Social studies				
Foreign language				
Physical education and health				
Career technical				
Electives				

*List specific courses or course numbers in the designated subject area students will take each year.

Dates Reviewed:_____

Comments:_____

_____

_____

_____

_____

_____

FORM 9.2   Unit of Credit Checklist

Name: _____   Graduation year:_____

_____ Total units required for selected program of study

NOTE: A = First Semester Course   B = Second Semester Course

English (_____Units Required)

☐ 9A   ☐ 10A   ☐ 11A   ☐ 12A   ☐ Other: _____
☐ 9B   ☐ 10B   ☐ 11B   ☐ 12B   ☐ Other: _____

Math (_____Units Required)

☐ Algebra 1A   ☐ Geometry A   ☐ Algebra 2A   ☐ Other:_____
☐ Algebra 1B   ☐ Geometry B   ☐ Algebra 2B   ☐ Other:_____
☐ Adv Alg/Trig A   ☐ Algebra 3A   ☐ Calculus A
☐ Adv Alg/Trig B   ☐ Algebra 3B   ☐ Calculus B

Science (_____Units Required)

☐ Intro Physics A   ☐ Biology A   ☐ Physics A   ☐ Chemistry A   ☐ Anatomy A
☐ Intro Physics B   ☐ Biology B   ☐ Physics B   ☐ Chemistry B   ☐ Anatomy B
☐ Other: _____
☐ Other: _____

Social Studies (_____ Units Required)

☐ World History A   ☐ American History A   ☐ Citizenship/Civics   ☐ Psychology
☐ World History B   ☐ American History B   ☐ Economics   ☐ Psychology
☐ Sociology   ☐ World Geography   ☐ Other_____
☐ Sociology   ☐ World Geography   ☐ Other_____

Physical Education (_____Units Required)

☐ Health/Safety   ☐ Personal Fitness

☐ Foreign Language (_____Units Required)

☐ Spanish 1A   ☐ Spanish 2A   ☐ German 1A   ☐ French 1A   ☐ Other: _____
☐ Spanish 1B   ☐ Spanish 2B   ☐ German 1B   ☐ French 1A   ☐ Other: _____

☐ Electives (_____Units Required)

1)_____   3) _____   5)_____   7)_____
2)_____   4) _____   6)_____   8)_____

☐ Other:_____

FORM 9.3 **Work-Based Student Evaluation**

Student name:_____ Date:_____

Job Site:_____

Task(s):

_____

_____

_____

_____

_____

Levels of Performance

Areas	Excellent 4 = Points	Satisfactory 3 = Points	Needs Improvement 2 = Points	Unsatisfactory 0 = Points	Total
Uses time card					
Demonstrates good hygiene and neat appearance					
Follows directions					
Greets employer appropriately					
Begins work immediately					
Remains on task					
Ask for more work/begins a new task when completed					
Leaves worksite appropriately					

Comments:

_____

_____

_____

_____

_____

Source: Adapted with permission from Jeromy Williams, Learning Specialist, Harlem High School.

FORM 9.4   Student's Critique of Job Site

Student name:_____   Date:_____

Job site:_____   Job coach:_____

Directions: Please answer the questions below:

1. What did you like about the job site?

_____

_____

2. What did you dislike about the job site?

_____

_____

3. Do the requirements of this job match your interests?   Yes or No

_____

_____

4. Do the requirements of this job match your abilities?   Yes or No

_____

_____

5. Are there any other skills needed to obtain this type of job?   Yes or No

_____

_____

6. Is this a realistic employment goal for you?   Yes or No

If yes, identify tentative job goal:

_____

_____

_____

_____

Source: Adapted with permission from Jeromy Williams, Learning Specialist, Harlem High School.

RESOURCE 9.1 Students With Disabilities Preparing for Postsecondary Education: Know Your Rights and Responsibilities

As a student with a disability leaving high school and entering postsecondary education, will I see differences in my rights and how they are addressed?

Yes. Section 504 and Title II protect elementary, secondary and postsecondary students from discrimination. Nevertheless, several of the requirements that apply through high school are different from the requirements that apply beyond high school. For instance, Section 504 requires a school district to provide a free appropriate public education (FAPE) to each child with a disability in the district's jurisdiction. Whatever the disability, a school district must identify an individual's education needs and provide any regular or special education and related aids and services necessary to meet those needs as well as it is meeting the needs of students without disabilities.

Unlike your high school, your postsecondary school is not required to provide FAPE. Rather, your postsecondary school is required to provide appropriate academic adjustments as necessary to ensure that it does not discriminate on the basis of disability. In addition, if your postsecondary school provides housing to nondisabled students, it must provide comparable, convenient and accessible housing to students with disabilities at the same cost.

Other important differences you need to know, even before you arrive at your postsecondary school, are addressed in the remaining questions.

May a postsecondary school deny my admission because I have a disability?

No. If you meet the essential requirements for admission, a postsecondary school may not deny your admission simply because you have a disability.

Do I have to inform a postsecondary school that I have a disability?

No. However, if you want the school to provide an academic adjustment, you must identify yourself as having a disability. Likewise, you should let the school know about your disability if you want to ensure that you are assigned to accessible facilities. In any event, your disclosure of a disability is always voluntary.

What academic adjustments must a postsecondary school provide?

The appropriate academic adjustment must be determined based on your disability and individual needs. Academic adjustments include modifications to academic requirements and auxiliary aids and services, for example, arranging for priority registration; reducing a course load; substituting one course for another; providing note takers, recording devices, sign language interpreters, extended time for testing and, if telephones are provided in dorm rooms, a TTY in your dorm room; and equipping school computers with screen-reading, voice recognition or other adaptive software or hardware.

In providing an academic adjustment, your postsecondary school is not required to lower or effect substantial modifications to essential requirements. For example, although your school may be required to provide extended testing time, it is not required to change the substantive content of the test. In addition, your postsecondary school does not have to make modifications that would fundamentally alter the nature of a service, program or activity or would result in undue financial or administrative burdens. Finally, your postsecondary school does not have to provide personal attendants, individually prescribed devices, readers for personal use or study, or other devices or services of a personal nature, such as tutoring and typing.

If I want an academic adjustment, what must I do?

You must inform the school that you have a disability and need an academic adjustment. Unlike your school district, your postsecondary school is not required to identify you as having a disability or assess your needs.

Your postsecondary school may require you to follow reasonable procedures to request an academic adjustment. You are responsible for knowing and following these procedures. Postsecondary schools usually include, in their publications providing general information, information on the procedures and contacts for requesting an academic adjustment. Such publications include recruitment materials, catalogs and student handbooks, and are often available on school Web sites. Many schools also have staff whose purpose is to assist students with disabilities. If you are unable to locate the procedures, ask a school official, such as an admissions officer or counselor.

When should I request an academic adjustment?

Although you may request an academic adjustment from your postsecondary school at any time, you should request it as early as possible. Some academic adjustments may take more time to provide than others. You should follow your school's procedures to ensure that your school has enough time to review your request and provide an appropriate academic adjustment.

Do I have to prove that I have a disability to obtain an academic adjustment?

Generally, yes. Your school probably will require you to provide documentation that shows you have a current disability and need an academic adjustment.

What documentation should I provide?

Schools may set reasonable standards for documentation. Some schools require more documentation than others. They may require you to provide documentation prepared by an appropriate professional, such as a medical doctor, psychologist or other qualified diagnostician. The required documentation may include one or more of the following: a diagnosis of your current disability; the date of the diagnosis; how the diagnosis was reached; the credentials of the professional; how your disability affects a major life activity; and how the disability affects your academic performance. The documentation should provide enough information for you and your school to decide what is an appropriate academic adjustment.

Although an Individualized Education Program (IEP) or Section 504 plan, if you have one, may help identify services that have been effective for you, it generally is not sufficient documentation. This is because postsecondary education presents different demands than high school education, and what you need to meet these new demands may be different. Also in some cases, the nature of a disability may change.

If the documentation that you have does not meet the postsecondary school's requirements, a school official must tell you in a timely manner what additional documentation you need to provide. You may need a new evaluation in order to provide the required documentation.

Who has to pay for a new evaluation?

Neither your high school nor your postsecondary school is required to conduct or pay for a new evaluation to document your disability and need for an academic adjustment. This may mean that you have to pay or find funding to pay an appropriate professional to do it. If you are eligible for services through your state vocational rehabilitation agency, you may qualify for an evaluation at no cost to you. You may locate your state vocational rehabilitation agency through this Department of Education Web page: http://www.ed.gov/parents/needs/speced/resources.html.

(Continued)

Once the school has received the necessary documentation from me, what should I expect?

The school will review your request in light of the essential requirements for the relevant program to help determine an appropriate academic adjustment. It is important to remember that the school is not required to lower or waive essential requirements. If you have requested a specific academic adjustment, the school may offer that academic adjustment or an alternative one if the alternative also would be effective. The school may also conduct its own evaluation of your disability and needs at its own expense.

You should expect your school to work with you in an interactive process to identify an appropriate academic adjustment. Unlike the experience you may have had in high school, however, do not expect your postsecondary school to invite your parents to participate in the process or to develop an IEP for you.

What if the academic adjustment we identified is not working?

Let the school know as soon as you become aware that the results are not what you expected. It may be too late to correct the problem if you wait until the course or activity is completed. You and your school should work together to resolve the problem.

May a postsecondary school charge me for providing an academic adjustment?

No. Furthermore, it may not charge students with disabilities more for participating in its programs or activities than it charges students who do not have disabilities.

What can I do if I believe the school is discriminating against me?

Practically every postsecondary school must have a person—frequently called the Section 504 Coordinator, ADA Coordinator, or Disability Services Coordinator—who coordinates the school's compliance with Section 504 or Title II or both laws. You may contact this person for information about how to address your concerns.

The school also must have grievance procedures. These procedures are not the same as the due process procedures with which you may be familiar from high school. However, the postsecondary school's grievance procedures must include steps to ensure that you may raise your concerns fully and fairly and must provide for the prompt and equitable resolution of complaints.

School publications, such as student handbooks and catalogs, usually describe the steps you must take to start the grievance process. Often, schools have both formal and informal processes. If you decide to use a grievance process, you should be prepared to present all the reasons that support your request.

If you are dissatisfied with the outcome from using the school's grievance procedures or you wish to pursue an alternative to using the grievance procedures, you may *file a complaint* against the school with OCR or in a court. You may learn more about the OCR complaint process from the brochure How to File a Discrimination Complaint with the Office for Civil Rights, which you may obtain by contacting us at the addresses and phone numbers below, or at http://www.ed.gov/ocr/docs/howto.html.

Source: U.S. Department of Education, Office for Civil Rights (2002).

RESOURCE 9.2	Work Behavior Training Strategies for Vocational Training for Students With Disabilities

1. Start with *initial orientation* to task, environment, materials, appropriate dress and expectations: outcomes.

2. *Design training sessions for success.* Prior to beginning a work session discuss what will be done and what the reinforcement will be. The reinforcement needs to be tangible and accessible.

3. *Identify expected behaviors* (vocational and social) in order to maximize efficient use of time allotted to do task. This should be reviewed frequently. This should be reinforced on the job whenever possible.

4. Be sure to set goals that the student will be able to reach (accessible) and the reinforcement is immediate (tangible) and it's something that motivates the student.

5. Once behavioral obstacles are identified, *develop behavior plan* to insure consistency amongst staff in addressing these behaviors.

6. Use *verbal agreements or contracts* when setting up what the task and reinforcement will be. Use verbal and visual reminders during the task if the student is getting distracted, tired or losing motivation to complete the work agreement. For example: After working for one hour we will take a coffee break, take a walk to get the mail, rest, fill out your time sheet so you get paid for the work done.

7. Prior to start of each task, based on task analysis, demonstrate appropriate operation/execution of task in slow *graduated* steps. (Well thought out) During training take nothing for granted no matter how simple the task might appear. (Backward chaining).

8. *Teach one task at a time.* Backward chaining: Complete a task sequence with the student and have them be responsible for the last piece in the task. During this time the staff person is doing the other parts of the task and explaining the task " getting the whole picture" Once the student has mastered a step, add the next step, and so on until the student is doing all steps of the task.

9. Through *observation* make note of any physical, cognitive and social deficits and be ready to adapt the job and/or develop compensatory strategies.

10. Use *written or picture task cards* to help with memory and sequencing of the task procedure. Possibly, have a check off sheet that the student can use to check off each step as it has been completed. This gives the student a visual guide to see their progress and how close they are to completing the task (helps deal with fatigue).

11. Develop *weekly schedules* to be distributed to and discuss with students.

12. Ratio of one teacher/trainer to two students (1:1 even better).

(Continued)

RESOURCE 9.2 (Continued)

13. Be extremely sensitive to *safety issues.* (i.e.. allergies, medications, physical sensitivities and limitations etc.)

14. Always be certain that necessary materials and equipment are: 1.) available at the beginning of the work period, and 2.) that students, with assistance when necessary, put all materials back in appropriate storage area.

15. Use *common sense* when assigning job sites.

16. As trainers it is essential that you are *well organized* and fully understand expected outcomes.

17. Try and treat students as workers not children.

18. *Data collection* is very important.

19. Try not to intervene immediately, using common sense. Allow student some time to either work out the problem or ask for assistance.

20. Comments made daily should be concise and relative to weaker areas. *Be specific,* NOT general. From these comments goals and objectives with emerge and subsequently tightening up you training program. Again, DO NOT assign too many tasks.

21. *Be consistent* with developing organizational and teaching strategies, students learning will be enhanced.

22. When teaching a task, keep it *specific, simple, demonstrate, monitor and then intervene.*

23. *Practice with and repetition of activities,* as well as feedback on performance, will strengthen the student's confidence to do the job.

24. Most importantly focus a lot on behavior in a *new environment* coupled with new expectations—you might discover different aspects/behaviors relative to students.

25. *Focus* primarily, where necessary, *on behavior.* Vocational skills will emerge as behaviors are controlled.

26. Each day should start with *review of training.* If appropriate, follow up discussion is very helpful.

27. When you are instructing always *ask questions* particularly during orientation to the job.

28. Very Important: As you *observe* students working try and determine need for use of OT, PT, speech , etc.

Source: From Paula Bliss, M.Ed., Special Education Teacher; http://www.paulabliss.com/trainstrategies.htm. Used with permission.

RESOURCE 9.3 **Job Accommodations for People With Mental Retardation (MR) or Other Developmental Disabilities (DD)**

COGNITIVE LIMITATIONS

Reading

- Provide pictures, symbols, or diagrams instead of words.
- Read written information to employee or provide written information on audiotape.
- Use voice output on computer.
- Use Reading Pen on single words.
- Use line guide to identify or hi-light one line of text at a time.

Writing

- Provide templates or forms to prompt information requested.
- Allow verbal response instead of written response.
- Allow typed response instead of written response.
- Use voice input and spell-check on computer.
- Use a scribe to write the employee's response.
- Provide ample space on forms requiring written response.
- Use voice activated recorder to record verbal instructions.

Calculations

- Allow use of large-display or talking calculator and use counter or ticker.
- Make pre-counted or pre-measured poster or jig.
- Provide talking tape measure and liquid level indicators.
- Mark the measuring cup with a "fill to here" line.

Organization

- Minimize clutter and color-code items or resources.
- Provide A-B-C and 1-2-3 chart.
- Divide large tasks into multiple smaller tasks.
- Use symbols instead of words and use print labels instead of hand-written labels.

Time Management

- Provide verbal prompts (reminders).
- Provide written or symbolic reminders.
- Use alarm watch or beeper.
- Use jig for assembly to increase productivity.
- Arrange materials in order of use.
- Use task list with numbers or symbols.

(Continued)

- Avoid isolated workstations.
- Provide space for job coach.
- Provide additional training or retraining as needed.

GROSS AND FINE MOTOR LIMITATIONS

Computer Use

- Use keyguard.
- Use alternative input devices such as speech recognition, trackball, and joystick.

Telephone Use

- Use large-button phone.
- Use phone with universal symbols (fire, police, doctor).
- Use phone with speed-dial, clearly labeled.
- Use receiver holder.
- Use headset.

Workstation Use

- Place anti-fatigue mats at workstation.
- Use motorized scooter.
- Use stools at workstations.
- Move items within reach.
- Provide frequent rest breaks.

Tool Use

- Use ergonomic tools, handle buildups, or other tool adaptations.
- Use orthopedic writing aids.
- Use grip aids.
- Use jig or brace.

SOCIAL INTERACTION

- Implement a structure of positive feedback.
- Use visual performance charts.
- Provide tangible rewards.
- Use coworkers as mentors and provide sensitivity training (disability awareness) to all employees.
- Use Employee Assistance Program (EAP).
- Provide job coach and use training videos to demonstrate appropriate behavior in workplace.
- Model appropriate social skills such as where to eat, when to hug, how to pay for coffee, and how to ask for help.

Source: Adapted from Job Accommodations Network (2008, n.d.).

10

Developing a Plan for Professional Learning

Habit 7: Sharpen the Saw

—Stephen Covey

Stephen Covey's "Habit 7: Sharpen the Saw" accurately depicts the need for the new teacher to develop a solid plan for professional learning. Covey (1992) states, "If you don't improve and renew yourself constantly, you'll fall into entropy, closed systems and styles. At one end of the continuum is entropy (everything breaks down), and at the other end is continuous improvement, innovation, and refinement" (p. 47). The development of a solid plan is essential in order for both beginning and veteran teachers to keep abreast of new instructional techniques, strategies, and programs that impact student learning and achievement; to acquire knowledge of current trends in special and general education; and to obtain information pertaining to legal developments in the profession that could impact students and programs. Professional learning is typically defined in the field of education as any course of action taken by a school employee for the purpose of increasing his or her skills in a particular academic area or knowledge of a specific educational topic. The landscape of special education is in a constant state of change, and the new teacher must assume personal responsibility for devising a plan for continuous improvement, one that will enable him or her to survive and thrive in the profession. In a time when the education profession as a whole is being held under a high-powered microscope, special education teachers throughout the country are finding their programs and services being scrutinized for productivity and effectiveness. Teachers who constantly "sharpen the saw" will find themselves to be on the cutting edge of the profession and in a continually progressing state of professional and personal growth. In this chapter, six strategies are presented that will assist the new teacher on his or her professional learning journey.

STRATEGY 1: FORMULATE A PROFESSIONAL DEVELOPMENT PLAN

The authors recommend that the beginning teacher begin developing a professional development plan prior to the start of each school year. The plan should include short- and long-term professional goals, a timeline for goal completion, and note the teacher's particular areas of interest. The plan should also include any professional learning or training needed to perform his or her current job effectively or to contribute to his or her school's current improvement initiatives. A completed professional development plan can assist the new teacher in performing a self-assessment at the end of each school year and serve as a record of professional pursuits and activities over a period of time. The plan should be placed in the teacher's portfolio (see Strategy 2) at the end of each school year.

Materials or Resources

Form 10.1 Professional Development Plan

STRATEGY 2: DEVELOP A PROFESSIONAL PORTFOLIO

The development of a professional portfolio is critical for all educators who are seeking employment or documenting personal growth in the field. The portfolio is a tool that teachers can use to showcase personal attributes, skills, and activities and to highlight their accomplishments as professional educators. Electronic portfolios are becoming more popular than traditional hard copy due to the convenience of the Internet and the ease with which Web page portfolios can be modified and updated. The authors recommend that the reader update and review his or her portfolio on a regular basis and reflect on the artifacts that have been collected during his or her journey.

Materials or Resources

Form 10.2 Portfolio for the Professional Educator

STRATEGY 3: JOIN A PROFESSIONAL ORGANIZATION

The authors suggest that the new special education teacher join at least one professional education organization. Often, these organizations distribute valuable information to their members through magazines, newsletters, journals, Web sites, or all of these; provide members with liability coverage; provide the new teacher with networking opportunities; and conduct annual conferences at the state or national level. The authors strongly recommend that new teachers attend at least one professional conference a year. Professional conferences for educators typically follow a general format that includes at least one general session with a keynote speaker, a variety of small group sessions on specific topics, and numerous how-to workshops that engage participants in interactive learning activities. The authors suggest that teachers review all conference information in advance and plan a daily agenda that will maximize their conference experience. Conference brochures can often be obtained in advance by visiting the sponsoring organization's Web site. Conferences can be viewed as one-stop resource centers that provide numerous opportunities to exchange ideas, materials, and resources with other educators and possibly obtain professional learning or continuing education credit. Professional learning credit can be used for recertification in some states. The authors have created a form designed to be used as a planning guide to ensure that one maximizes his or her opportunities and time at any conference. A list of professional organizations is provided in Resource 10.4. The authors have included a list of additional organizations that can provide the beginning special education teacher with resource information pertaining to specific diseases or health conditions.

Materials or Resources

Form 10.3 Conference Planning Guide

Resource 10.1 The Special Education Teacher's Guide to Professional Organizations

STRATEGY 4: READ PROFESSIONAL JOURNALS AND BOOKS

The reading of educational journals and books on a regular basis is necessary to stay current in the profession. The media centers of most schools have professional resources available for faculty and staff members. If the new teacher finds his or her school's media center lacking in a particular area, however, he or she should check with the media specialist to determine if additional resources can be ordered. The Internet is a valuable tool for locating and purchasing current books and other resource material. Some of the larger bookstore chains carry extensive inventories online and provide speedy delivery of purchases. The authors suggest summarizing all material that is found to be of particular interest and maintaining the information in a three-ring notebook that is organized by subject areas or topics and allows for quick referencing or reviewing by the reader. A list of current periodicals and books pertaining to special and regular education can be found in Resources 10.2 and 10.3.

Materials or Resources

Resource 10.2 The Special Education Teacher's Guide to Professional Periodicals

Resource 10.3 The Special Education Teacher's Guide to Professional Books

Resource 10.4 Web Sites for Special Education Teachers

STRATEGY 5: ENROLL IN ADVANCED COLLEGE COURSES OR PROFESSIONAL LEARNING CLASSES

The authors recommend that the new teacher enroll in advanced college courses or local professional learning classes offered through the school system once a comfort level has been reached in his or her current teaching position. Often, new college graduates are eager to "have it all" and misjudge the amount of personal energy required for a new teaching job and pursuing a graduate degree. The authors recommend that the new teacher wait approximately three years before pursuing a new degree or adding an additional area of certification. Finally, the authors remind the reader that college courses are usually more expensive; professional learning classes, however, are usually offered within the school system at low or no cost to school employees, scheduled after school hours or during the summer, and give credit toward recertification.

STRATEGY 6: PARTICIPATE IN A PROFESSIONAL LEARNING COMMUNITY

Participating in a professional learning community at the school level is another strategy that can assist the new teacher with his or her professional growth. In a professional learning community, teachers and school stakeholders work together for the common good of the students. Richard DuFour (2004) found that a professional learning community "requires the school staff to focus on learning rather than teaching, work collaboratively on matters related to learning, and hold itself accountable for the kind of results that fuel continual improvement" (p. 11). Historically, school systems have developed professional learning programs that are global by design and primarily focused on identified or perceived needs of the entire system; often, however, these programs do not necessarily address the individual needs of schools or of teachers and staff members. School administrators and teachers are taking action by creating professional learning communities within their schools. Eamonn O'Donovan (2007) found that,

> Working as a Professional Learning Community makes it more likely that teachers will ask the right questions about student learning: What do students need to know? How do we assess learning? What do we do when students do not learn? What do we do when students have already mastered expectations? (p. 95)

The authors find that the most significant benefit of participating in a professional learning community is that the team's focus is always on "the work" and getting student results. This type of focus will result in teacher growth over a period of time.

FORM 10.1   Professional Development Plan

School year: _____

Special education teacher: _____

Certification number: _____ Expiration date: _____

Licensure number: _____ Expiration date: _____

Certification area/grade level (list): _____

_____

Short-Range Professional Goals (Completion Within One Year):

Professional Goal	Completion Date
1.	
2.	
3.	
4.	
5.	

Long-Range Professional Goals (Completion Within Five Years):

Professional Goal	Completion Date
1.	
2.	
3.	
4.	
5.	

FORM 10.2   Portfolio for the Professional Educator

PORTFOLIO CONTENTS CHECKLIST

_____ Cover page

_____ Table of contents

_____ Personal résumé

_____ Philosophy of education

_____ Graduate coursework

_____ Practicum and student teaching experiences

_____ Descriptions of special projects or programs

_____ Technology applications and skills

_____ Professional learning activities

_____ Copies of awards or certificates

_____ Copies of certification and/or licensures

_____ Copies of letters or recommendations

PORTFOLIO TIPS

A special education teacher's professional portfolio should:

1. be placed in a three-ring notebook with dividers and/or tabs.

2. be neat, clean, well organized, error free, and have a consistent appearance.

3. contain copies of only important documents.

4. contain current information.

FORM 10.3   Conference Planning Guide

Conference name: _____

Conference dates: _____ Conference location: _____

Sponsoring organization: _____

Conference cost:

    Registration fee: $ _____

    Hotel accommodations: $ _____

    Travel/mileage: $ _____

    TOTAL EXPENSE: $ _____

Conference theme or objectives:

_____

_____

_____

_____

_____

Personal Conference Schedule

Date	Time	Session Title	Location

RESOURCE 10.1   The Special Education Teacher's Guide to Professional Organizations

American Association on Intellectual and
    Developmental Disabilities
444 N. Capitol Street NW, Suite 846
Washington, DC 20001-1512
Telephone: 800-424-3688
Fax: 202-87-2193
Web site: www.aaidd.org

American Council of the Blind
1155 15th Street NW, Suite 1004
Washington, DC 20005
Telephone: 202-67-5081
Toll free: 800-424-8666
Fax: 202-467-5085
Web site: www.acb.org

American Federation of Teachers
555 New Jersey Avenue NW
Washington, DC 20001
Telephone: 202-879-4400
Web site: www.aft.org

American Juvenile Arthritis Organization
P. O. Box 7669
Atlanta, GA 30357-0669
Toll free: 800-283-7800
Web site: www.arthritis.org/ajao

American Speech-Language-Hearing Association
2200 Research Boulevard
Rockville, MD 20850-3289
Members: 800-498-2071
Non-Members: 800-638-8255
Fax: 301-296-8580
Email: actioncenter@asha.org
Web site: www.asha.org

The ARC of the United States
1010 Wayne Avenue, Suite 650
Silver Spring, MD 20910
Telephone: 301-565-3842 or 800-433-5255
Fax: 301-565-3843 or 301-565-5342
National Policy Email: info@thearc.org
Public Policy Email: gaoinfo@thearc.org
Web site: www.thearc.org

Association for Persons in Supported Employment
1627 Monument Avenue
Richmond, VA 23220
Telephone: 804-278-9187
Fax: 804-278-9377
Email: apse@apse.org
Web site: www.apse.org

Autism Society of America
7910 Woodmont Avenue, Suite 300
Bethesda, MD 20814-3067
Telephone: 301-657-0881
Toll free: 800-3AUTISM (800-3280-8476)
Web site: www.autism-society.org

Council for Children with Behavioral Disorders
    (CCBD)
P. O. Box 24246
Stanley, KS 66223
Fax: 913-239-0550
Web site: www.ccbd.net

Council for Exceptional Children (CEC)
Ballston Plaza Two
1110 North Glebe Road, Suite 300
Arlington, VA 22201-5704
Telephone: 800-224-6830
Fax: 703-264-9494
Web site: www.cec-sped.org

Division for Early Childhood (DEC)
Division of Council for Exceptional Children
27 Fort Missoula Road, Suite 2
Missoula, MT 59804
Telephone: 406-543-0872
Fax: 406-543-0887
Web site: www.dec-sped.org

Division for Learning Disabilities
Division of Council for Exceptional Children
1110 North Glebe Road, Suite 300
Arlington, VA 22201-5704
Telephone: 1-888-CEC-SPED (1-888-232-7733)
Telephone: 706-620-3660
Fax: 703-264-9494

Division on Career Development and Transition (DCDT)
Division of Council for Exceptional Children
1920 Association Drive
Reston, VA 20191
Robert Miller, President
Telephone: 703-620-3660
Fax: 703-264-9494

Division on Visual Impairment (DVI)
C/O Council for Exceptional Children
1920 Association Drive
Reston, VA 20191-1589
Roseanna Davidson, President
Telephone: 703-620-3660
Fax: 703-264-9494
Web site: www.cecdvi.org

Foundation for Exceptional Children (FEC)
Center for Human Development
332 Birnie Avenue
Springfield, MA 01107
Telephone: 413-733-6624
Fax: 413-439-2109
Email: info@chd.org

Learning Disabilities Association of America
4156 Library Road
Pittsburgh, PA 15234-1349
Telephone: 412-341-1515
Fax: 412-344-0224
Web site: www.ldanatl.org

Muscular Dystrophy Association–USA
National Headquarters
3300 E. Sunrise Drive
Tucson, AZ 85718
Telephone: 800-572-1717
Web site: www.mda.org

National Alliance of Black School Educators (NABSE)
310 Pennsylvania Ave. SE
Washington, DC 20003
Telephone: 202-608-6310
Fax: 202-608-6319
Web site: www.nabse.org

National Association of Councils on Developmental Disabilities
225 Reinekers Lane, Suite 650-B
Alexandria, VA 22314
Telephone: 703-739-4400
Fax: 703-739-6030
Email: info@nacdd.org
Web site: www.nacdd.org

National Association of Early Childhood Teacher Educators (NAFCTE)
Web site: www.naecte.org

National Down Syndrome Society
666 Broadway
New York, NY 10012
Telephone: 800-221-4602
Fax: 212-979-2873
Email: info@ndss.org
Web site: www1.ndss.org

National Education Association (NEA)
1201 16th Street NW
Washington, DC 20036-3290
Telephone: 202-833-4000
Fax: 202-822-7974
Web site: www.nea.org

Spina Bifida Association of America
4590 MacArthur Blvd. NW
Washington, DC 20007
Telephone: 202-944-3285 or 1-800-621-3141
Fax: 202-944-3295
Email: sbaa@sbaa.org
Web site: www.sbaa.org

United Cerebral Palsy
1660 L Street NW, Suite 700
Washington, DC 20036
Telephone: 202-776-0406
Telephone: 800-872-5827
Fax: 202-776-0414
Email: info@ucp.org
Web site: www.ucp.org

RESOURCE 10.2   The Special Education Teacher's Guide to Professional Periodicals

Autism Asperger's Digest

Behavioral Disorders

Education and Training in Mental Retardation

Exceptional Child Education Resources

Exceptional Children

Exceptional Parent

Focus on Exceptional Children

Journal of Learning Disabilities

Journal of Special Education

Journal of Speech and Hearing Services in the Schools

Journal of Visual Impairment & Blindness

Learning Disability Quarterly

Phi Delta Kappan

Preventing School Failure

Remedial and Special Education

Teaching Exceptional Children

RESOURCE 10.3 **The Special Education Teacher's Guide to Professional Books**

Assessing Students With Special Needs

Authors: James A. McLoughlin et al.
Publisher: Prentice Hall PTR
Date: March 2004

Best Teaching Practices for Reaching All Learners

Author: Randi Stone
Publisher: Corwin Press
Date: March 2004

Building Classroom Discipline

Author: C. M. Charles
Publisher: Allyn & Bacon
Date: April 2004

Children Don't Come With an Instruction Manual: A Teacher's Guide to Problems That Affect Learners

Author: Wendy Moss
Publisher: Teachers College Press
Date: April 2004

The Classroom of Choice: Giving Students What They Need and Getting What You Want

Author: Jonathan C. Erwin
Publisher: Association for Supervision & Curriculum Development
Date: May 2004

The Complete Guide to Asperger's Syndrome

Author: Tony Attwood
Publisher: Jessica Kingsley Publishers
Date: May 2008

Concise Encyclopedia of Special Education: A Reference for the Education of the Handicapped and Other Exceptional Children and Adults

Authors: Cecil R. Reynolds et al.
Publisher: John Wiley
Date: March 2004

Creating Inclusive Classrooms: Effective and Reflective Practices

Author: Spencer J. Salend
Publisher: Prentice Hall PTR
Date: May 2004

(Continued)

RESOURCE 10.3 (Continued)

Dealing With Difficult Parents and With Parents in Difficult Situations

Author: Todd Whitaker & Douglas J. Fiore
Publisher: Eye On Education
Date: 2001

Differentiated Instructional Strategies

Authors: Gayle H. Gregory & Carolyn Chapman
Publisher: Corwin Press
Date: 2007

The General Educator's Guide to Special Education: A Resource Handbook for All Who Teach Students With Special Needs

Author: Jody L. Maanum
Publisher: Peytral
Date: January 2004

How to Differentiate Instruction in Mixed Ability Classrooms (2nd ed.)

Author: Carol Ann Tomlinson
Publisher: Association for Supervision and Curriculum Development
Date: May 2004

Managing the Adolescent Classroom: Lessons From Outstanding Teachers

Author: Glenda Beamon Crawford
Publisher: Corwin Press
Date: May 2004

One-Minute Discipline: Classroom Management Strategies That Work

Author: Arnie Bianco
Publisher: John Wiley
Date: October 2002

Promising Practices Connecting Schools to Families of Children With Special Needs

Author: Diana B. Hiatt-Michael
Publisher: Information Age
Date: January 2004

Sensational Kids: Hope and Help for Children With Sensory Processing Disorders

Authors: Lucy Jane Miller & Doris A. Fuller
Publisher: Penguin Group USA
Date: January 2007

Special Educational Needs: A Resource for Practitioners

Author: Michael Farrell
Publisher: Corwin Press
Date: February 2004

Teaching With Love and Logic: Taking Control of the Classroom

Authors: Jim Fay & David Funk
Publisher: Corwin Press
Date: February 2004

Technology and the Diverse Learner: A Guide to Classroom Practice

Authors: Marty Bray et al.
Publisher: The Love and Logic Press Inc.
Date: 1995

To Understand: New Horizons in Reading Comprehension

Author: Ellyn Oliver Keene
Publisher: Heinemann
Date: January 2008

Understanding by Design

Authors: Grant Wiggins & Jay Cliché
Publisher: Association for Supervision and Curriculum Development
Date: 1998

Very Young Children With Special Needs: A Formative Approach for the Twenty-First Century

Authors: Vikki F. Howard et al.
Publisher: Merrill College Press
Date: February 2004

Vocational and Transition Services for Adolescents With Emotional and Behavioral Disorders: Strategies and Best Practices

Authors: Michael Bullis et al.
Publisher: Research Press
Date: January 2004

What Great Teachers Do Differently: 14 Things That Matter Most?

Author: Todd Whitaker
Publisher: Eye On Education
Date: 2004

What Every Teacher Should Know About Classroom Management and Discipline

Author: Donna E. Walker Tileston
Publisher: Corwin Press
Date: October 2003

Wrightslaw: From Emotions to Advocacy: The Special Education Survival Guide

Authors: Peter W. D. Wright & Pamela Darer Wright
Publisher: Harbor House Law Press
Date: January 2006

RESOURCE 10.4   Web Sites for Special Education Teachers

All Kids Grieve
    www.allkidsgrive.org/

American Association on Mental Retardation
    www.aamr.org/

American Speech-Language-Hearing Association
    www.asha.org/default.htm

Association for Supervision and Curriculum Development (ASCD)
    www.ascd.org

Autism Society of America
    www.autism-society.org/site/PageServer

CHADD (Children and Adults With Attention Deficit/Hyperactivity Disorder)
    www.chadd.org

Council for Exceptional Children
    www.cec.sped.org

Council of Administrators of Special Education
    www.casecec.org/

Division for Learning Disabilities
    www.dldcec.org

Federal No Child Left Behind Act of 2001
    www.ed.gov/nclb/landing.jhtml#

Learning Disabilities Association of America
    www.ladnatl.org/

Middle School Students and School Life
    www.middleweb.com/ContntsStudn.html

National Board for Professional Teaching Standards
    www.nbpts.org/

National Education Association Crisis Communications and Toolkit
    www.nea.org/crisis/index.html

National Transition Alliance for Youth with Disabilities
    http://cecp.air.org/teams/stratpart/nta.asp

Quick Training Aid: School-Based Crisis Intervention
    www.smph.psych.ucla.edu/qf/crisis_qt/

Resource A

Emergencies in the School Setting

The majority of new special education teachers will enter into their first teaching positions with the skills necessary to meet the academic needs of their students; however, there is a spectrum of noninstructional situations that the beginning teacher could possibly encounter during his or her first year. Emergencies in the school setting are the most complex of these noninstructional situations and often require the new teacher to react immediately and with extreme decisiveness. The following are examples of school emergencies:

- A student becomes physically ill
- A student experiences a mental health episode
- A natural disaster occurs
- An act of violence occurs

All schools should have a safety plan book that outlines procedures and protocols pertaining to specific emergency situations. The authors advise the beginning teacher to obtain and read this book prior to the start of the school year. In addition, a school employee is usually assigned the position of safety officer to ensure that these policies are being followed as directed. The new teacher should address all questions or concerns to the school's safety officer. Resource A includes a list of possible school emergencies and supplemental forms to support selected topics.

SECTION 1: PHYSICAL HEALTH ISSUES OF STUDENTS

The classroom teacher is usually the first adult to respond to ill students and must be able to assess their physical condition at the scene and determine the proper course of action without hesitation. Most schools have standard procedures for handling ill students in the school setting. Most likely, these procedures call for the teacher to escort the student to the school nurse or the main office. The teacher must inform the school's administration whenever a medical emergency occurs and complete all required school forms that document the incident. The authors suggest that the teacher meet the nurse assigned to the school and discuss any specific medical issues or concerns pertaining to his or her students before the first day of school. The nurse can provide a wealth of information and updated first-responder's guidelines for specific medical situations. The authors suggest that teachers of medically fragile students request access to an immediate communication device or system to be used to request immediate assistance. Typically, modern classrooms have emergency call buttons that connect the teacher to the main office when pushed; however, the teacher may need another device such as a two-way radio to carry when he or she is in areas outside of the classroom. The authors recommend that the new teacher take the following actions before the new school year begins:

1. Review the school system's policies and procedures that specifically address how teachers are to handle medical emergencies in the school environment.

2. Request updated medical information from parents at the beginning of each school year. A medical history form (Form A.1) has been included.

3. The teacher should review the form and note all significant medical problems. The teacher should develop an emergency medical plan for all students who have a significant medical problem or condition (e.g., seizures, allergic reaction to bee stings, and asthma; Form A.2). A copy of the plan should be kept in the school's main office.

4. The teacher should complete a report after each medical incident (Form A.3).

5. The teacher should inform all school personnel who will have a significant amount of contact with the student of his or her medical condition or problem (e.g., inform the physical education teacher if the student has asthma).

6. The teacher must remember to keep a log of all medical incidents that occur during the school year (Form A.4). Theses forms need to be kept in a secure location that is easily accessible for teacher or paraprofessional to reference.

Common Student Illnesses:

- Asthma

- Diabetes Mellitus

- Seizures:
  a. Absence seizure
  b. Grand mal seizure

SECTION 2: MENTAL HEALTH ISSUES OF STUDENTS

Teachers who work with adolescents must be able to recognize the warning signs of suicide and substance abuse. Most school systems have specific protocols and procedures for reporting students who are threatening to commit suicide or appear to have a substance abuse problem. The new teacher must review these documents prior to the start of the school year. If a teacher suspects or has confirmed knowledge that a student is in danger, he or she must follow his or her school's protocol which typically includes informing the student's parents, the school counselor, and a school administrator.

SECTION 3: REVIEW OF NATURAL DISASTERS

During the past five years, natural disasters have been responsible for hundreds of deaths and millions of dollars in property damage in the United States. The beginning teacher must know the appropriate actions to take if a natural disaster occurs during school hours. The school's safety plan book should clearly outline the teacher's actions for each type of emergency. It is imperative that the teacher always review the classroom evacuation plan with his or her students on the first day of school. In addition, the school will conduct evacuation drills as directed by the state guidelines, and the teacher must treat the drills as though they were in response to a real event. The authors have provided the reader with a list of various types of natural disasters.

- **Earthquake**
- **Fire**
- **Flood**
  Important Terms to Know:

  a. **Flood Watch or Flashflood Watch**—Flooding may happen soon. Stay tuned to the radio or television news for more information. If you hear a flashflood warning, talk to an adult immediately!

  b. **Flood Warning**—You may be asked to leave the area. A flood may be happening or will be very soon. Tell an adult if you hear a flood warning. If you have to leave the area, remember to bring your Disaster Supply Kit and make arrangements for your pets.

  c. **Flashflood Warning**—A flashflood is happening. Get to high ground right away.

- **Hurricane**
- **Tornado**
  Important Terms to Know:

  a. **Tornado Watch**—Tornadoes are possible. Stay tuned to the radio or television news.

  b. **Tornado Warning**—A tornado has been sighted. Take shelter immediately!

Adapted from FEMA for Kids: The Disaster Area. (n.d.)

SECTION 4: ACTS OF VIOLENCE

The new teacher will discover that schools have not been left untouched by the increasing number of violent acts committed by juveniles. In response to some of the most horrific acts of violence committed by students in America, school systems have developed comprehensive emergency management plans to use during dangerous situations. The authors urge the beginning teacher to seek out the school's safety officer and request an orientation to the plan prior to the start of the school year. The new teacher must ask the school's safety officer for the specific teacher actions for the following situations:

a. An explosion in the building.

b. A radiological, hazardous, or toxic material accident.

c. A weapon on campus.

d. A hostage or terrorist event.

e. An intruder on campus.

In addition, the teacher must know when to employ the following primary response actions during an emergency:

a. Evacuation

b. Lockdown

c. Shelter-in-place

FORM A.1 *Medical History*

Student name:_____   School year:_____

Date of birth:_____   Grade:_____

Home telephone number:_____

Mother/guardian's name:_____

    Work telephone number:_____

    Cell telephone number:_____

    E-mail address:_____

Father/guardian's name:_____

    Work telephone number:_____

    Cell telephone number:_____

    E-mail address:_____

Emergency contact:_____

      Name   Relationship   Telephone number

Student's medical problem (please be specific):

_____

_____

_____

Current medication (dosage and time of administration):

_____

_____

_____

Allergies:

_____

_____

_____

Parent/guardian signature:_____   Date:_____

FORM A.2   Emergency Medical Plan

Student name:_____   School year:_____

Date of birth:_____   Grade:_____

Home telephone number:_____

Medical problem or condition: (please be specific)

_____

_____

_____

_____

_____

_____

_____

_____

Emergency plan of action:

_____

_____

_____

_____

_____

_____

_____

_____

_____

_____

Parent's/guardian's signature:_____   Date:_____

Teacher's signature:_____   Date:_____

School administrator's signature:_____   Date:_____

Copy on file in main school office and/or with school nurse: _____Yes   or   _____No

---

FORM A.3   Medical Incident Report

Date:_____

Student name:_____   Grade:_____

Accident or illness description:

_____

_____

_____

_____

_____

_____

_____

_____

_____

_____

Teacher or paraprofessional response:

_____

_____

_____

_____

_____

_____

_____

_____

_____

_____

_____

_____

_____

Date and time of parent notification:_____

Teacher's signature:_____

FORM A.4   Medical Incident Log

School year:_____

Date	Student Name	Description of Injury or Illness	Teacher's Response

RESOURCE A.1   Classroom "Go-Kit" Supplies

Clipboard with lists of:

- All classroom students

    - Students with special needs and description of needs (i.e., medical issues, prescription medicines, dietary needs), marked confidential

    - Classroom personnel

    - School emergency procedures

- Whistle

- Hat or vest for teacher identification

- First-aid kit with instructions

- Pens and paper

- Age-appropriate student activities (such as playing cards, checkers, inflatable ball, etc.)

Source: U.S. Department of Education (2006, July).

RESOURCE A.2   Recommended First-Aid Supplies

The authors recommend the following medical supplies for the classroom's first-aid kit:

- Adhesive strip bandages, assorted sizes

- Adhesive tape, 1- and 2-inch rolls

- Antibiotic skin ointment

- Chemical ice pack

- Cotton balls

- Disposable latex gloves

- Elastic bandages, 2-, 3-, and 4-inch width

- Gauze pads: 2 × 2 and 4 × 4

- Hydrogen peroxide

- Non-adhering dressing

- Scissors

- Tweezers

- Hand sanitizer

- Antiseptic wipes

- Cotton swabs

Resource B

Stress Management for the First-Year Teacher

The first-year teacher will quickly discover that the profession of special education can be both physically and emotionally demanding. Stress is a fact of life for most teachers; the enormous caseloads, continuous documenting of student progress, meeting the emotional and academic needs of students, and the threat of litigation, however, are some of the contributing factors to the job-related stress experienced by teachers in the special education profession. Seaward (as quoted in Massey, 1998) defined stress as "the inability to cope with a perceived or real (or imaginary) threat to one's mental, physical, emotional, and spiritual well-being which results in a series of physiological responses" (p. 1). The simple definition of stress is the body's reaction to the demands placed on it. A certain amount of stress is helpful to keep individuals focused on the job or problem; stress that impedes the teacher's ability to function in the school setting and serve students effectively is counterproductive, however. The authors believe that if the teacher experiences prolonged, elevated levels of job-related stress, the result could be job burnout.

The beginning teacher must be able to manage workplace stress effectively in order to survive the entire school year. The special education teacher must identify his or her stress source and then implement effective stress management strategies. The following are sources of stress identified by Zunker (1994) that the authors found to be most applicable to the special education teaching profession:

- Conditions of work (unpleasant work environment, necessity to work fast, and excessive and inconvenient hours)
- The work itself (perception of job as uninteresting, repetitious, overloaded, and demanding)
- Supervision (unclear job demands, close supervision with no autonomy, and scant feedback from supervisors)
- Role ambiguity (lack of clarity about one's job and scope of responsibilities)
- Group stressor (insufficient group cohesiveness and poor group identity in the organization)
- Organizational structure (too bureaucratic or too autocratic)

The authors provide the reader with suggestions for stress management (Resource B.1) at the end of the chapter.

Finally, the authors suggest that teachers who continue to have difficulty with stress management enroll in staff development courses designed to teach stress management strategies to school employees. The authors strongly urge the beginning teacher to contact his or her school administrator or special education director if all attempts at stress reduction have failed.

RESOURCE B.1   Tips for Stress Management

- Schedule moments of reflection and stress management daily. Rise early, and allow more time for personal reflection before the workday begins.

- Recognize stressful situations quickly, analyze personal feelings, breathe deeply, and loosen muscles.

- When stress builds, use deep breathing techniques and progressive muscle relaxation exercises to reduce tension.

- Learn the strategies of conflict management.

- Learn and be willing to say "No."

- Ask for help.

- Focus on an immediate goal, and work on it until it is completed.

- Try a new activity.

- Talk to significant other.

- Pay attention to health, diet, and sleep needs.

- Exercise daily.

- Leave your teaching at school.

- Do not schedule all your leisure time.

- Pursue a project or hobby.

- Find a friend.

- Do not procrastinate.

- Do not feel that you must do everything.

- Keep a "things to do" list.

- Recognize and accept your limitations.

- Learn to tolerate and forgive.

- Learn to plan.

- Be a positive person.

- Learn to play.

- Rid yourself of worry.

Source: Georgia Association of Educators (1998).

Resource C

Support Organizations for Students

Adults, Adolescents, and Children with Attention-Deficit/Hyperactivity Disorder (CHADD)

8181 Professional Place, Suite 150
Landover, MD 20785
Phone, toll-free: 800-233-4050
Phone, local: 301-306-7070
Web site: www.chadd.org

American Amputee Foundation

P.O. Box 94227
North Little Rock, AR 72190
Phone: 501-835-9290
Fax: 501-835-9292

American Association of the Deaf-Blind

8630 Fenton Street, Suite 121
Silver Spring, MD 20910-3803
TTY Phone: 301-495-4402
Voice Phone: 301-495-4403
Fax: 301-495-4404

American Association on Intellectual and Developmental Disabilities

444 North Capitol Street, NW, Suite 846
Washington, DC 20001-1512
Phone: 1-800-424-3688
Fax: 202-387-2193

Attention Deficit Information Network

58 Prince Street
Needham, MA 02492

Phone: 781-455-9895
Web Site: www.addinfonetwork.org

Council for Learning Disabilities (CLD)

P.O. Box 4014
Leesburg, VA 20177
Phone: 571-258-1010
Web site: www.cldinternational.org

Division for Learning Disabilities

Council for Exceptional Children
1110 N. Glebe Road, Suite 300
Arlington, VA 22201-5704
Phone, toll free: 888-232-7733; 800-224-6830
Phone: 866-915-5000 (V/TTY)
E-mail: cec@cec.sped.org
Web site: www.dldcec.org/

Job Accommodations Network

Phone, toll free: 1-800-526-7234 in the United States
Phone, toll free: 1-800-526-2262 in Canada
Web site: http://janweb.icdi.wvu.edu

Learning Disabilities Association of America (LDA)

4156 Library Road
Pittsburgh, PA 15234
Phone: 412-341-1515
Publications available in Spanish
E-mail: info@ldaamerica.org
Web site: www.ldaamerica.org

(Continued)

(Continued)

Autism Society of America

7910 Woodmont Avenue, Suite 300

Bethesda, MD 20814-3067

Phone: 301-657-0881

Phone, toll free: 1-800-3AUTISM (1-800-328-8476)

Web site: www.autism-society.org/

MAAP Services for Autism, Asperger's, and PDD

P.O. Box 524

Crown Point, IN 46308

E-mail: info@maapservices.org

Web: www.maapservices.org

Phone: 219-662-1311

Fax: 219-662-0638

Attention Deficit Disorder Association (ADDA)

P.O. Box 543

Pottstown, PA 19464

Phone: 484-945-2101

Web site: www.add.org

National Down Syndrome Society

666 Broadway

New York, NY 10012

Phone, toll free: 800-221-4602

Phone, local: 212-979-2873

E-mail: info@ndss.org

The National Information Center for Children and Youth with Disabilities

P.O. Box 1492

Washington, DC 20013-1492

Phone, toll free: 800-695-0285

Fax: 202-884-8441

E-mail: nichcy@aed.org

Web site: www.nichcy.org

Resource D

Guide to Locating Instructional Materials

Academic Therapy Publications

20 Commercial Boulevard
Novato, CA 94949-6191
Telephone: 800-422-7249
Fax: 888-287-9975
Web site: www.academictherapy.com/

The Bureau for At-Risk Youth

P.O. Box 9120
Plainview, NY 11803-9020
Telephone: 800-431-1934
Fax: 888-803-3908
Web site: www.at-risk.com

Channing L. Bete Co., Inc.

One Community Place
South Deerfield, MA 01373-0200
Telephone: 800-477-4776
Fax: 800-499-6464
Web site: www.channing-bete.com

Curriculum Associates, Inc.

Corporate Headquarters
P.O. Box 2001
North Billerica, MA 01862-9914
Telephone: 800-225-0248
Fax: 800-366-1158
Web site: www.curriculumassociates.com

A. D. D. Warehouse

300 NW 70th Avenue, Suite 102
Plantation, FL 33337
Telephone: 800-233-9273
Fax: 954-792-8545
Web site: www.addwarehouse.com

Educators Publishing Service

P.O. Box 9031
Cambridge, MA 02139-9031
Telephone: 800-435-7728
Fax: 888-440-2665
Web site: www.epsbooks.com

Prufrock Press

P.O. Box 8813
Waco, TX 76714-8813
Telephone: 800-998-2208
Fax: 800-240-0333
Web site: www.prufrock.com

Remedia Publications

15887 North 76 Street, Suite 120
Scottsdale, AZ 85260
Telephone: 800-826-4740
Fax: 602-661-9901
Web site: www.rempub.com

(Continued)

(Continued)

Research Press

P.O. Box 9177
Champaign, IL 61826
Telephone: 800-519-2707
Fax: 217-352-1221
Web site: www.researchpress.com

School Scrabble Program

P.O. Box 700
Greenport, NY 11944
Web site:
www.scrabbleassoc.com/school

Greenwood Publishing Group, Inc.

88 Post Road West
Westport, CT 06881
Telephone: 203-226-3571
Fax: 203-222-1502
Web site: www.greenwood.com

Incentive Publications

2400 Crestmoor Road, Suite 211
Nashville, TN 37215
Telephone: 800-421-2830
Web site: www.incentivepublications.com

Psychological and Educational Tests Division, Stoelting Company

620 Wheat Lane
Wood Dale, IL 60191
Telephone: 630-860-9700
Fax: 630-860-9775
Web site: www.stoeltingco.com/stoelting/templates/99/homepageStoelting.aspx?storename=Psychological

Kaplan Concepts for Exceptional Children

1310 Lewisville-Clemmons Road
Lewisville, NC 27023-0609
Telephone: 800-334-2014
Fax: 800-452-7526
Web site: www.kaplanco.com

Lakeshore Learning Materials

2695 East Dominquez Street
Carson, CA 90749
Telephone: 800-428-4414
Fax: 310-537-5403
Web site: www.lakeshorelearning.com

Macmillan/McGraw-Hill Glencoe

220 East Danieldale Road
Desoto, TX 75115
Telephone: 800-442-9685
Fax: 972-228-1982
Web site: www.mhschool.com

PCI Educational Publishing

2800 NE Loop 410, Suite 105
San Antonio, TX 78218-1525
Telephone: 800-594-4263
Fax: 888-259-8284
Web site: www.pcicatalog.com

Slosson

P.O. Box 544
East Aurora, NY 14052-0280
Telephone: 888-756-7766
Fax: 800-655-3840
Web site: www.slosson.com

SRA/McGraw-Hill

220 East Danieldale Road
DeSoto, TX 75115-2490
Telephone: 800-843-8855
Fax: 214-228-1982

Teacher Ideas Press

Libraries Unlimited
P.O. Box 6926
Portsmouth, NH 03802-6926
Telephone: 800-255-5800
Fax: 877-231-6980
Web site: www.lu.com

Resource E

Education Terminology

Activating prior knowledge: "Helping learners connect to concepts about to be taught by using activities that relate to or determine the level of their existing knowledge." (PlasmaLink Web Services, 2007)

Adequate yearly progress (AYP): "An individual state's measure of yearly progress toward achieving state academic standards. 'Adequate Yearly Progress' is the minimum level of improvement that states, school districts and schools must achieve each year." (U.S. Department of Education, 2004)

Alternative certification: "Most teachers are required to have both a college degree in education and a state certification before they can enter the classroom. *No Child Left Behind* encourages states to offer other methods of qualification that allow talented individuals to teach subjects they know." (U.S. Department of Education, 2004)

At-risk student: Typically, students identified as "at-risk" are not progressing in the general education curriculum at the same rate as their peers. Limited cognitive abilities, excessive absenteeism, discipline issues, and social/emotional issues are a few of the most common factors that affect a student's academic performance therefore causing him or her to be at risk for school failure and/or dropout.

Audio-visuals: "Includes many categories of educational materials including: posters, paintings, slides, videos, films, audio tapes, and videotapes." (PlasmaLink Web Services, 2007)

Authentic assessment: "Alternative tests which assess student ability to solve problems and perform task under simulated 'real life' situations. It measures student responses which demonstrate what students think, do and have become. These outcomes are recorded during normal classroom involvement. Teachers may use hand-held computer scanners that scan the students' bar coded name and responses, then transfer the information into a computer later." (KJOS Ministries, n.d.)

Benchmark assessment: "Benchmark Assessments are reliable and valid, standards-based assessments administered to a whole-group or individual at regular intervals. The assessment results can be used to determine student growth and student performance relative to statewide grade-level achievement expectations." (Pennsylvania Training & Technical Assistance Network, n.d.)

Charter school: "Charter schools are independent public schools designed and operated by educators, parents, community leaders, educational entrepreneurs, and others. They are sponsored by designated local or state educational organizations that monitor their quality and effectiveness but allow them to operate outside of the traditional system of public schools." (U.S. Department of Education, 2004)

Collaborative learning: "Any kind of work that involves two or more students." (PlasmaLink Web Services, 2007)

Corrective action: "When a school or school district does not make yearly progress, the state will place it under a 'Corrective Action Plan.' The plan will include resources to improve teaching, administration, or curriculum. If a school continues to be identified as in need of improvement, then the state has increased authority to make any necessary, additional changes to ensure improvement." (U.S. Department of Education, 2004)

Differentiated instruction: "Differentiated instruction is responsive instruction. It occurs as teachers become increasingly proficient in understanding their students as individuals, increasingly comfortable with the meaning and structure of the disciplines they teach, and increasingly expert at teaching flexibly in order to match instruction to student need with the goal of maximizing the potential of each learner in a given area." (Tomlinson, 2003, pp. 2–3)

Disaggregated data: "'Disaggregate' means to separate a whole into its parts. In education, this term means that test results are sorted into groups of students who are economically disadvantaged, from racial and ethnic minority groups, have disabilities, or have limited English fluency. This practice allows parents and teachers to see more than just the average score for their child's school. Instead, parents and teachers can see how each student group is performing." (U.S. Department of Education, 2004)

Formative assessment: "Formative assessment is part of the instructional process. When incorporated into classroom practice, it provides the information needed to adjust teaching and learning while they are happening." (Garrison & Ehringhaus, n.d.)

Graphic organizer: "Graphic organizers are visual frameworks to help the learner make connections between concepts." (PlasmaLink Web Services, 2007)

Guided practice: "Guided Practice is a form of scaffolding. It allows learners to attempt things they would not be capable of without assistance." (PlasmaLink Web Services, 2007)

Inclusion: "Inclusion is the process of providing all students with the opportunity to participate in the school community regardless of their individual strengths or limitations." (PlasmaLink Web Services, 2007)

Progress monitoring: "Progress monitoring is the ongoing process of collecting and analyzing data to determine student progress toward general outcomes and making instructional decisions based on ther review and analysis of student data." (U.S. Department of Education, n.d.)

Public school choice: "Students in schools identified as in need of improvement will have the option to transfer to better public schools in their districts. The school districts will be required to provide transportation to the students. Priority will be given to low-income students." (U.S. Department of Education, 2004)

Response to intervention: "Response to Intervention (RTI) involves maximizing student achievement by monitoring student progress to make data-based instructional decisions for students. While RTI varies in its methodologies, a common model is based on implementation of universal, secondary, and tertiary interventions (Kamps & Greenwood, 2005; Fuchs & Fuchs, 2006; Vaughn, 2003). Universal interventions involve providing high quality core instruction to students in regular education classrooms. Secondary interventions involve more intensive small group instruction, and tertiary interventions are even more intensive and are often provided by an interventionist or special educator." (Office of Special Education and Rehabilitative Services, 2007)

Summative assessments: "Summative Assessments are given periodically to determine at a particular point in time what students know and do not know." (Garrison & Ehringhaus, n.d.)

Title I: "The first section of the ESEA, Title I refers to programs aimed at America's most disadvantaged students. Title I Part A provides assistance to improve the teaching and learning of children in high-poverty schools to enable those children to meet challenging State academic content and performance standards. Title I reaches about 12.5 million students enrolled in both public and private schools." (U.S. Department of Education, 2004)

Unsafe school choice option: "Students who attend persistently dangerous public schools or have been victims of violent crime at school are allowed to transfer to a safer public school." (U.S. Department of Education, 2004)

References

Introduction

Daugherty, R. F. (2003). Reflections from first-year teachers: References from Sallie Mae award winners [Electronic version]. *Education, 123*(3), 458–462.

Gordon, S. P. & Maxey, S. (2000). *How to help beginning teachers succeed.* Alexandria, VA: Association of for Supervision & Curriculum Development.

Mandel, S. (2006). What new teachers really need. *Educational Leadership, 63*(6), 66–69.

Whitaker, S. D. (2001). Supporting beginning special education teachers. *Focus on Exceptional Children, 34*(4), 1–18.

Chapter 1

Daugherty, R. F. (2003). Reflections from first-year teachers: References from Sallie Mae award winners [Electronic version]. *Education, 123*(3), 458–462.

Fore, C., Martin, C., & Bender, W. (2002). Teacher burnout in special education: The causes and the recommended solutions. *High School Journal, 86*(1), 36–45.

French, N. K. (2002). Maximize paraprofessional services for students with learning disabilities. *Intervention in School and Clinic, 38*(1), 50–55.

Friend, M., & Bursuck, W. (2002). *Including students with special needs: A practical guide for classroom teachers.* Boston, MA: Allyn & Bacon.

Sabella, R. A., & Booker, B. L. (2003). Using technology to promote your guidance and counseling program among stake holders [Electronic version]. *Professional School Counseling, 6,* 206–214.

Salend, S. J. (2001). *Creating inclusive classrooms: Effective and reflective practices.* Upper Saddle River, NJ: Prentice Hall.

U.S. Department of Education. (2004). *Building the legacy: Idea 2004.* Statute: Title/I/602: Retrieved April 10, 2008, from http://idea.ed.gov/explore/view/p/%2Croot%2Cstatute%2CI%2CA%2C602%2C

Chapter 2

Boehner, J. (2003). *No child left behind emphasizes results, expands options for children with special needs* [Fact Sheet]. Retrieved March 3, 2004, from House Education & the Workforce Committee Web site: http://edworkforce.house.gov/issues/108th/education/nclb/specialneeds.htm

Gearheart, B. R., Mullen, R. C., & Gearheart, C. J. (1993). *Exceptional individuals: An introduction.* Belmont, CA: Wadsworth.

Haraway, D. (2002). In their own words: The lessons we learn if we hear. *Preventing School Failure, 46*(2), 57–61.

IDEA '97 final regulations. (n.d.). Retrieved October 23, 2008, from http://www.specialed .us/discoveridea/idearegsmain.htm

Kaplan, H. I., Sadock, B. J., & Grebb, J. A. (1991). *Synopsis of psychiatry: Behavioral sciences, clinical psychiatry* (6th ed.). Baltimore, MD: Williams & Wilkins.

Mastropieri, M. A. (2001). Is the glass half full or half empty? Challenges encountered by first-year special education teachers [Electronic version]. *Journal of Special Education, 35*(2), 66–75.

Schildroth, A. N., & Karchmer, M. A. (1986). *Deaf children in America.* Austin, TX: Pro-Ed.

Smith, D. D., & Luckasson, R. (1992). *Introduction to special education teaching in the age of challenge.* Needham Heights, MA: Allyn & Bacon.

Chapter 3

Bureau of Jewish Education of San Francisco, the Peninsula, Marin and Sonoma Counties. (2006). *Special education handbook-models.* Retrieved October 16, 2008, from http:// www.bjesf.org/downloads/bje_specialedhandbook2006.pdf

Department of Education: Assistance to States for the Education of Children with Disabilities and Preschool Grants for Children with Disabilities, 71 Fed. Reg. No. 156 (2006) (to be codified at 34 C.F.R. Parts 300 and 301)

Polloway, E. A., Epstein, M. H., & Bursuck, W. D. (2003, April). Testing adaptations in the general education classroom: Challenges and directions. *Reading and Writing Quarterly, 19,* 189–192.

Rizzo, J. V., & Zabel, R. H. (1988). *Educating children and adolescents with behavioral disorders: An integrative approach.* Needham Heights, MA: Allyn & Bacon.

Smith, D. D., & Luckasson, R. (1992). *Introduction to special education teaching in the age of challenge.* Needham Heights, MA: Allyn & Bacon.

Chapter 4

Backes, C. E., & Ellis, I. C. (2003, May). The secret of classroom management. *Techniques,* pp. 22–25.

Discipline with dignity. (n.d.). Retrieved November 3, 2008, from Teacher Learning Center Web site: http://www.tlc-sems.com/Discipline-With-Dignity.aspx

Lewis, R. B., & Doorlag, D. H. (2003). *Teaching special students in general education classrooms* (6th ed.). Upper Saddle River, NJ: Merrill.

Love and logic: Kids don't come with an owner's manual. (2008). Retrieved November 3, 2008, from http://www.loveandlogic.com/

Marzano, R. J., & Marzano, J. S. (2003). The key to classroom management. *Educational Leadership, 61*(1), 6–13.

Miller, S., Wackman, S., Nunnally, E., & Miller, P. (1988). *Connecting with self and others.* Littleton, CO: Interpersonal Communication Programs.

Salend, S. J. (2001). *Creating inclusive classrooms: Effective reflective practices.* Upper Saddle River, NJ: Merrill Prentice Hall.

The three C's: Provide some encouragement. (n.d.). Retrieved November 3, 2008, from the Cooperative Discipline Overview Site: http://members.tripod.com/tkmoyer/ CooperativeDiscipline/id17.htm

Watson, S. (2008). *ABA: Applied behavior analysis.* Retrieved November 3, 2008, from the About.com Web site: http://specialed.about.com/od/specialedacronyms/g/aba.htm

Wong, H. (1991). *The effective teacher.* Sunnyvale, CA: Wong Publications.

Chapter 5

Georgia Department of Education. (2008). *So, what IS a standards-based classroom?* [PowerPoint Slide 3]. Available from http://www.tiftschools.com/Presentations/standards%20based%20classrooms.ppt

Levy, H. (2008). Meeting the needs of all students through differentiated instruction: Helping every child reach and exceed standards. *The Clearing House, 81*(4), 161–164.

Mercer, C. D., & Mercer, A. R. (1993). *Teaching students with learning problems.* New York: Macmillan.

Tanner, B. M., Bottoms, G., & Bearman, A. (2001). *Instructional strategies: How teachers teach matters.* Atlanta, GA: Southern Regional Education Board.

Thompson, M., & Thompson, J. (2003). *Learning-focused schools strategies notebook* [Workbook]. Boone, NC: Learning Concepts.

U.S. Department of Education. (1996, Spring). What are promising ways to assess student learning? *Improving America's school: A newsletter on issues in school reform.* Retrieved April 5, 2004, from http://www.ed.gov/pubs/IASA/newsletters/assess/pt.3.html

Walker, M. (2007). *Differentiated instruction* [PowerPoint slides]. Available from http://www.ed.gov/teachers/how/tools/initiative/summerworkshop/walker/walker.pdf

Chapter 6

Berger, E. (1995). *Parents as partners in education: Families and schools working together.* Englewood Cliffs, NJ: Prentice Hall.

Black, S. (2005, October). Rethinking parent conferences. *American School Board Journal,* pp. 46–48.

Hackmann, D. (1997). *Student-led conferences at the middle level* (Report No. ED407171). Champaign, IL: ERIC Clearinghouse on Elementary and Early Childhood Education.

Miller, S., Wackman, S., Nunnally, E., & Miller, P. (1988). *Connecting with self and others.* Littleton, CO: Interpersonal Communication Programs.

Million, J. (2005, April). Getting teachers set for parent conferences. *The Education Digest,* pp. 54–56.

Minke, K., & Anderson, K. (2003). Restructuring routine parent–teacher conferences: The families–school conference model. *The Elementary School Journal, 104*(1), 49–69.

Morehead, M. A. (2001). *Dealing with the anger of parents.* Retrieved January 8, 2004 from New Mexico State University Web site: http//education.nmsu.edu/departments/academic/ci/morehead/handouts/angry.html

Shea, I. M., & Bauer, A. M. (1991). *Parents and teachers of children with exceptionalities.* Needham Heights, MA: Allyn & Bacon.

Chapter 7

Browder, D., Flowers, C., Ahlgrim-Delzell, L., Karvonen, M., Spooner, F., & Algozzine, R. (2004). The alignment of alternate assessment content with academic and functional curricula. *The Journal of Special Education, 37*(4), 211–223.

Buros Institute of Mental Measurement Test Reviews Online. (n.d.). Retrieved April 23, 2004, from http://buros.unl.edu/buros/jsp/reviews.jsp?item=06000003

Canter, A. (1998). Understanding test scores: A handout for teachers. *National Association of School Psychologists,* pp. 119–120

Classroom assessment. (n.d.). Retrieved April 21, 2008, from http://fcit.usf.edu/assessment/basic/basica.html

Cummings, K., Allison, R., Atkins, T., & Cole, C. (2008). *Response to intervention. Teaching Exceptional Children, 40*(4), 24–31.

Department of Education: Assistance to States for the Education of Children with Disabilities and Preschool Grants for Children with Disabilities, 71 Fed. Reg. No. 156 (2006) (to be codified at 34 C.F.R. Parts 300 and 301)

Johnson, E., & Arnold, N. (2007). Examining an alternate assessment. *Journal of Disability Policy Studies, 18*(1), 23–31.

Linn, J. E., & Gronlund, M. A. (1995). *Measurement and assessment in teaching.* Englewood Cliffs, NJ: Prentice Hall.

Mehrens, W. A., & Lehmann, I. J. (1987). *Using standardized tests in education.* White Plains, NY: Longman.

Roeber, E. (2002). *Setting standards on alternate assessments* (Synthesis Report 42). Minneapolis: University of Minnesota, National Center on Educational Outcomes. Retrieved April 26, 2008, from http://education.umn.edu/NCEO/OnlinePubs/Synthesis42.html

Sweetland, R. C., & O'Connor, W. (Eds.). (1984). *Tests: A comprehensive reference for assessments in psychology, education and business.* Kansas City, MO: SKS Associates.

Guidelines for determining modifications for use on state and district assessments for students with disabilities. (1998, July). [Technical Assistance Paper No. FY 1999-2]. Tallahassee: Florida Department of Education, Division of Public Schools and Community Education, Bureau of Instructional Support and Community Services.

Thurlow, M. L., Elliott, J. L., & Ysseldyke, J. E. (1998). *Testing students with disabilities: Practical strategies for complying with district and state requirements.* Thousand Oaks, CA: Corwin Press.

U.S. Department of Education. (2004). *Building the legacy: Idea 2004.* Statute: Title /I/ 602: Retrieved April 10, 2008, from http://idea.ed.gov/explore/view/p/%2Croot%2Cstatute%2CI%2CA%2C602%2C

Chapter 8

Department of Education: Assistance to States for the Education of Children with Disabilities and Preschool Grants for Children with Disabilities, 71 Fed. Reg. No. 156 (2006) (to be codified at 34 C.F.R. Parts 300 and 301)

Mager, R. F. (1984). *Preparing instructional objectives.* Belmont, CA: Pitman Learning.

Mason, C. Y., McGahee-Kovac, M., & Johnson, L. (2004). How to help students lead their IEP meetings. *Teaching Exceptional Children, 36*(3), 18–25.

U.S. Department of Education. (2004, July). *Overview: Four pillars of NCLB.* Retrieved April 23, 2008, from http://www.ed.gov/nclb/overview/intro/4pillars.html

Chapter 9

Bliss, P. (2003, November 3). STW units. *Paula's special education resources.* Retrieved April 30, 2004, from http://www.paulabliss.com/stwgoals.htm

CEC Today. (1999). *A primer on IDEA and its regulations, 5*(7), 5.

Gil, L. A. (2007). Bridging the transition gap from high school to college: Preparing students with disabilities for a successful postsecondary experience. *Teaching Exceptional Children, 40*(2), 12–15.

Job Accommodations Network. (2008). *Fact sheet series: Job accommodations for people with intellectual or developmental disabilities.* Retrieved October 27, 2008, from http://www.jan.wvu.edu/media/employmentmrfact.doc

Job Accommodations Network. (n.d.). *Step 3: Select the job function cognitive abilities.* Retrieved October 23, 2008, from http://www.jan.wvu.edu/soar/mr/3_cog.html

Kohler, P. D., & Field, S. (2003). Transition-focused education: Foundation for the future. *Journal of Special Education, 37*(3), 174–183.

Mager, R. F. (1984). *Measuring instructional results or got a match?* (2nd ed.). Belmont, CA: Lake Publishing.

Queen, J. A. (2002). *Student transitions from middle to high school: Improving achievement and creating a safer environment.* Larchmont, NY: Eye on Education.

Scarborough, J., & Gilbride, D. (2006). Developing relationships with rehabilitation counselors to meet the transition needs of students with disabilities. *Professional School Counseling, 10*(1), 25–33.

U.S. Department of Education, Office for Civil Rights. (2002). *Students with disabilities preparing for postsecondary education: Know your rights and responsibilities.* Washington, DC: Author.

Wehman, P. (1996). *Life beyond the classroom* (2nd ed.). Baltimore, MD: Brookes.

Chapter 10

Covey, S. R. (1992). *Principle-centered leadership.* New York: Simon & Schuster.

DuFour, R. (2004). What is a "professional learning community"? *Educational Leadership, 61*(8), 6–11.

O'Donovan, E. (2007, March). Professional learning communities. *District Administration: The Magazine of School District Management.* Retrieved April 20, 2008, from http://www.districtadministration.com/ViewArticle.aspx?articleid=1106

Resource A

U.S. Department of Education. (2006, July). *Helpful hints for school emergency management: Emergency "go-kits."* Retrieved April 19, 2008, from http://rems.ed.gov/views/documents/HH_GoKits.pdf

U.S. Department of Homeland Security. (n.d.). *Ready kids: Know the facts.* Retrieved April 19, 2008, from http://www.ready.gov/kids/step3/index.html

Resource B

Georgia Association of Educators. (1998). *Avoiding burnout and staying healthy* [Online]. Available at http://smhp.psych.ucla.edu/qf/burnout_qt/avoidburn.pdf

Massey, M. S. (1998). *Promoting stress management: The role of the comprehensive school health programs.* Washington, DC: ERIC Clearinghouse on Teaching and Teacher Education. (ERIC Document Reproduction Service No. ED421480)

Zunker, V. G. (1994). *Career counseling: Applied concepts of life planning* (4th ed.). Pacific Grove, CA: Cole.

Resource E

Fuchs, D., & Fuchs, L. S. (2006). Introduction to response to intervention: What, why, and how valid is it? *Reading Research Quarterly, 41,* 92–99.

Garrison, C., & Ehringhaus, M. (n.d.). *Formative and summative assessments in the classroom.* Retrieved April 20, 2008, from http://www.nmsa.org/Publications/WebExclusive/Assessment/tabid/1120/Default.aspx

Kamp, D., & Greenwood, C. R. (2005). Formulating secondary-level reading interventions. *Journal of Learning Disabilities, 38,* 500–509.

KJOS Ministries. (n.d.). *Glossary of education terms.* Retrieved April 20, 2008, from http://www.crossroad.to/glossary/education.html

Office of Special Education and Rehabilitation Services. (2007). Retrieved November 3, 2008, from the Federal Register Online via GPO Access Web site: http://www.ed.gov/legislation/FedRegister/announcements/2007-1/032007a.html

Pennsylvania Training & Technical Assistance Network. (n.d.). *Benchmark assessment.* Retrieved April 20, 2008, from http://www.pattan.k12.pa.us/teachlead/Benchmark Assessment.aspx

PlasmaLink Web Services. (2007, October). *Glossary of instructional strategies.* Retrieved April 20, 2008, from http://glossary.plasmalink.com/glossary.html

Tomlinson, C. A. (2003). *Fulfilling the promise of the differentiated classroom.* Alexandria, VA: Association for Supervision and Curriculum Development.

U.S. Department of Education. (2004, July). *Glossary of terms.* Retrieved April 20, 2008, from http://www.ed.gov/nclb/index/az/glossary.html

U.S. Department of Education. (n.d.). *Accelerating student learning: Monitoring reading.* Retrieved October 16, 2008, from http://www.ed.gov/teachers/how/tools/initiative/summerworkshop/warkomski/edlite-slide006.html

Vaughn, S. (2003). *How many tiers are needed for response to intervention to achieve acceptable prevention outcomes.* Retrieved October 23, 2008, from The National Research Center on Learning Disabilities Web site: http://www.nrcld.org/symposium2003/vaughn/vaughn.pdf

Index